© 2008 York Associates

No part of this publication may be reproduced, stored in a retrieval system or transmitted in any form or by any means, electronic, mechanical, photocopying, recording, or otherwise, without the prior permission of the publishers. This book is sold subject to the condition that it shall not, by way of trade or otherwise, be lent, re-sold, hired out or otherwise circulated without the publisher's prior consent in any form of binding or cover than that in which it is published.

First edition 2008
Published by York Associates International Ltd.
Book and cover designed by Professor Brian Switzer, envision+, www.envisionplus.com
Illustrations by Jakob Behrends & Professor Brian Switzer
Paper: Profil Publish manufactured by Deutsche Papier; FSC, PEFC, Swan Label certified
Printed in Germany by Vereinigte Verlagsanstalten GmbH Niederlassung Konkordia/Wesel Kommunikation.

ISBN 978-1-900991-18-6

The publisher
The mission of York Associates is to help people to develop internationally. In addition to its publishing activities, it offers a wide range of training in management, communication, intercultural and language skills to private and public sector clients worldwide. It offers training and coaching to individuals and groups at its main training centre at Peasholme House, an eighteenth century town house close to the historic centre of York in the north of England, and in-house worldwide.

York Associates International Ltd.
Peasholme House, St Saviours Place
York YO1 7PJ, England
Tel: + 44 (0)1904 624246
Fax: + 44 (0)1904 646971
training@york-associates.co.uk
www.york-associates.co.uk

The Mindful International Manager
Competences for Working Effectively
across Cultures

Jeremy Comfort and Peter Franklin

Table of contents

Acknowledgements

Numerous people have helped to make this book possible and though our debt to many of them may be obvious in places, we nevertheless would like to thank them explicitly for the role they played – knowingly or unknowingly – in creating it.

We would like to thank the managers who were kind enough to give us the interviews we have used in the book. We have acknowledged them and the organisations they work for by name in the text and short biographies of them are included at the back of the book. In this connection, we would also like to thank Bob Dignen, Director of York Associates, who was responsible for conducting the interviews.

We are very grateful to those countless people working across cultures who over the years have enriched our workshops and courses with their experiences and insights and in that way unwittingly contributed to the book. Without their stimulation the book would have been much poorer.

We also express our thanks to all those fellow interculturalists and other writers, researchers and scholars whose insights we have benefited from and used. Their names appear in the text itself and in endnotes, and the particular books and articles we refer to are contained in the list of references at the end of the book. We acknowledge with special thanks our debt to Ellen J. Langer, the late William B. Gudykunst and Stella Ting-Toomey, whose work introduced us to the concept of mindfulness.

Finally, particular thanks go to Nigel Ewington and his colleagues at World-Work Ltd. for allowing us to make such liberal use of their International Profiler set of competences; to Janet Leonard and her colleagues at TMS Development International Ltd for allowing us to use the Team Management Profile; to Markus Haag for devising the glossary; to Professor Brian Switzer of HTWG Konstanz for designing such a striking book; and to Steve Flinders, Director of York Associates, for editing it.

Jeremy Comfort and Peter Franklin

Foreword

When Jeremy Comfort and Peter Franklin approached Henkel Learning Management with the aim of developing a programme which would support our intercultural and diversity training, we were happy and ready to cooperate in the production of 'Developing People Internationally (DPI)'. After all, York Associates had already successfully delivered intercultural communication skills training at Henkel for some time. We had also been looking for a tool which not only added a blended learning element to our training but also provided our language and communication trainers with a means of accomplishing that paradigm shift from language to skills training.

With the increasing internationalisation of Henkel – it is presently operating in 125 countries with 55,000 employees worldwide – we soon realised that the communication context was also changing. In addition to talking to external suppliers and customers, managers increasingly speak with colleagues from affiliates. In fact, about 80% of business interaction is in-company and business communication is about global strategy and structures, which dominate all company processes. Procedures have thus to be harmonized and coordinated worldwide. It doesn't require much imagination to understand how complex and difficult handling communication has become. Virtually all business areas are affected by it, from production to marketing, from research to human resources.

Our employees require communication and intercultural competence. Specifically this means they need strategies not only for clarifying, for reaching agreement, for influencing decisions, for negotiating meaning and for building commitment and trust, but also for exchanging and presenting information and explaining processes. York Associates' approach to intercultural communication training, supported by the new online programme 'Developing People Internationally (DPI)', has turned out to be a very helpful stepping-stone towards meeting these global and diverse management demands.

With this publication, Peter and Jeremy are taking another step on the road. The Mindful International Manager provides further support to our managers facing these complex demands. With its emphasis on reflection and observation, the book complements fully the DPI training initiative. It weaves theory and practice together with the emphasis on the latter so that both experienced and inexperienced managers can be guided through the many challenges of working internationally.

Gabriele Eilert-Ebke
Training Manager
Henkel AG&Co.KGaA, Düsseldorf

Chapter 0
About this book

This part of the book answers these questions

what does the book do?

what is meant by 'The Mindful International Manager'?

what is meant by 'competences for working effectively across cultures'?

what makes the book different from other books about working internationally?

who is the book for?

who is the book not for?

who are the writers of the book?

What does this book do?
The book not only *explains* cultural and individual differences in management values and behaviour. It also helps you to *handle* these differences.

It not only gives you the *knowledge* you need to understand things but it also describes the *skills* and *competences* you need to work effectively across cultures.

What is meant by 'The Mindful[1] International Manager'?
Mindful international managers:
> focus with understanding on the *context* and *process* of communication and cooperation as well as on their *outcome*;
> create understanding when communicating with people with backgrounds different from their own, for example, by
>> listening actively
>> modifying their language to make it more comprehensible
>> paraphrasing
>> testing their own understanding and
>> paying attention to non-verbal behaviour;
> pay attention to their own cultural and individual assumptions, values and norms;
> realise that these are only one set of guiding principles for action amongst many others;
> pay attention to what they can see of the cultural and individual assumptions, values and norms of the people with whom they are working;
> try to see the different cultures and situations they are in through the eyes and with the feelings of the people they are working with;
> take account of these different perspectives and feelings in their own actions and in their evaluations of people from different cultures.

What is meant by 'competences[2] for working effectively across cultures'?
We mean the
> knowledge,
> skills,
> attitudes,
> traits and
> motives
which research and experience have shown you need in order to be effective in international situations.

We describe these key intercultural competences so that you can reflect upon yourself and develop the competences which you think are important to you in your particular situation.

What makes this book different from other books about working internationally?
This book:
> places managers and the management situations they have to handle in their daily work at the centre of the stage;
> quotes the experiences and insights of practising international managers;
> not only describes differences and difficulties
> but also describes what skills and competences you need to handle them effectively;
> does not suggest that the challenges facing a manager working internationally are exclusively caused by differences in national or ethnic culture but also
> deals with the influence of organisational culture and
> emphasises the importance of the personality and preferences of the individual manager;
> avoids harmful stereotypes;
> is written with readers of English as a foreign language in mind. We have tried to use short sentences and paragraphs as well as simple grammar and vocabulary. We have included at the back of the book a glossary of words which are more difficult.
> tries to do without jargon. Where jargon is unavoidable, it is relatively transparent and easy to understand.

Who is this book for?
The Mindful International Manager is for
> the business traveller
> the expatriate manager
> anybody working in an international company alongside foreign colleagues, in a joint venture or in an international virtual team.

In short, if you are working internationally (or are about to do so) and you realise that things are not quite the same as they are at home but are not quite sure why that is so, then this book is for you.

Who is this book *not* for?
The book is *not* intended for *intercultural trainers and HR developers*: they should already be dealing with these things in their training seminars! Nor is it intended for *researchers or university teachers*. Although the book is based on knowledge and insights developed by researchers, they will probably not find it sufficiently detailed or technical.

Who are the writers of the book?

The book was written by Jeremy Comfort and Peter Franklin. They were both brought up and educated in Great Britain but since then have both had international and intercultural careers, living and / or working outside the U.K. (mainly in Europe) and with people from all over the world.

Despite this international context to their lives, their book inevitably reflects their particular view of the world. It also displays the Western orientation of the knowledge and insights they possess about culture, communication and management. Readers should be aware of this 'culture-centredness' because members of other cultures may well see the world differently.

Jeremy Comfort founded York Associates, UK, nearly thirty years ago with the mission to develop people internationally. He has trained and coached hundreds of individuals and teams who face the ever more complex challenges of working internationally. Jeremy is responsible for creating the Developing People Internationally approach, an innovative set of training materials, out of which this book has grown.

Peter Franklin is professor of intercultural business and management communication at Konstanz University of Applied Sciences, Germany. His teaching and research activities concern language, culture and communication in international business. Peter also advises and trains corporate clients, for example, in the areas of post-merger integration, international team building and intercultural management competence development.

Notes

1
Ting-Toomey (1999) and Gudykunst (2004, 4th ed) brought the concept of mindfulness to intercultural communication studies from psychology, where it was first elaborated on by Langer (1989, 1997). In the management field Thomas and Kerr (2003) underline the significance of mindfulness.

2
The key competences described are taken from the Worldwork Ltd set of competences for working effectively in international contexts. Based on a throrough review of the Western research literature from a variety of disciplines, the competency set and Worldwork's International Profiler tool offer a practical means for developing intercultural competence. Full details can be found at http://www.worldwork.biz.

Chapter 1
Home and away

This chapter focuses on

why the mindful manager needs to communicate more transparently when working internationally than when working at home

why it is important to understand the impact of culture on your behaviour and on the way you manage

how your behaviour and the way you manage can be the result of culturally determined values, beliefs and attitudes

how culture functions as an orientation system and gives its members identity and a sense of belonging

how we are all members of a number of different cultures at the same time

Core competences | 1.1

All managers achieve results through the people they manage and influence. Managing effectively across cultures is even more challenging than operating just in your own culture. Mindful international managers understand the challenges and are ready to deal with them.

At home, in a domestic environment, a lot of what we expect of the people we manage is unspoken – it is taken for granted. For example, a manager might say to someone in her team, "I'd like that report by next Monday", and the team member understands what she is saying about the finished state of the report and the urgency of the deadline. He understands because she has said it many times before and everyone in the team has a shared understanding of what is needed in this situation.

Of course, this does not mean that the report will arrive on time and in the right state! That also depends on the competence and motivation of the person writing the report. In a domestic context, we often do not surface our expectations of performance because we feel people understand them. The familiar context helps to get the message across.

What makes teams work well
Domestic teams often perform better than international ones, relying on this unspoken and shared understanding. But well-managed international teams have the potential to do better than home teams.

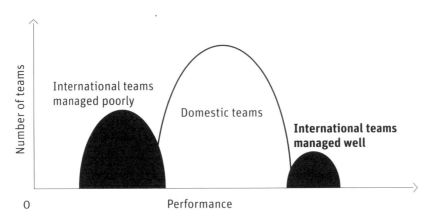

Adapted from Distefano and Maznevski (2000)

The *underlying* competences we need to make a team perform well are the same, whether we work at home or abroad.

The virtuous circle of team management competences.

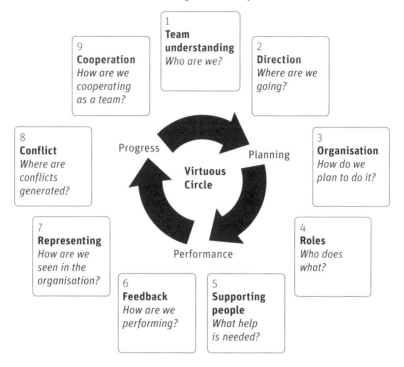

The DPI Model © York Associates 2007

1 Understanding your team: get to know team members and
the key players by building relationships.
2 Giving direction to the team: communicate common goals and benefits
clearly to gain team commitment.
3 Organising and coordinating resources (time, people, money):
plan and generate guidelines for working in the team.
4 Clarifying roles and responsibilities in the team:
ensure people know who does what.
5 Supporting the team and its members: consider the benefits of mentoring,
coaching, facilitating and networking.
6 Monitoring performance and giving feedback to the team: motivate
team members by giving and getting individual and team feedback.
7 Representing: promote the work of the team externally and
present and 'sell' the project.
8 Handling conflict: manage internal and external resistance and conflict.
9 Building a culture of cooperation: enable people to cooperate effectively
and move towards synergy.

As we go through the chapters in this book, we will be looking at these
management competences.

Surfacing expectations | 1.2

When they are working in an international environment, mindful managers do not assume that their teams and other stakeholders understand their expectations.

A U.S. manager, sitting in her office in Boston, emails an Italian colleague working in Milan. She writes: "I'd like that report by next Monday". The U.S. manager intends this as an urgent request for a finished report. But the Italian may understand this as a wish, not a request. He may not feel the urgency of the deadline at all.

When the report does not arrive, the U.S. manager's prejudice about 'unpunctual Italians' is confirmed. She phones her Italian colleague and expresses her frustration. This confirms the Italian's prejudice about 'pushy Americans'.

Mindful management of an international team means that you need to surface your expectations and expose your intentions much more transparently. If you do this, your performance and results will compare very well with those of your domestic team.

Cultural icebergs

Before managers communicate their specific expectations, it is important for them to reflect on the differences between their own organisational culture and the organisational cultures which their team members may be used to.

Many writers[1] have described organisational culture as an iceberg. Edgar Schein[2] breaks culture down into three parts:

1   Above the surface: features of the culture which you can see.
What do you notice first about the company's culture? What do you see when you first enter the building? What processes are in place?

2   Just below the surface: official norms and codes of conduct
What does the company communicate about its culture? What are its stated values? How does it expect its people to behave? What is its strategy, its philosophy? What are its goals?

3   Deep below the surface: hidden assumptions and truths
What have you discovered about the culture after you have worked there for some time? What are the unspoken beliefs?

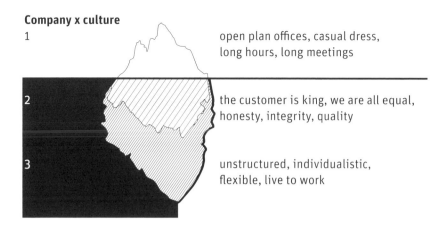

Company x culture

1 — open plan offices, casual dress, long hours, long meetings

2 — the customer is king, we are all equal, honesty, integrity, quality

3 — unstructured, individualistic, flexible, live to work

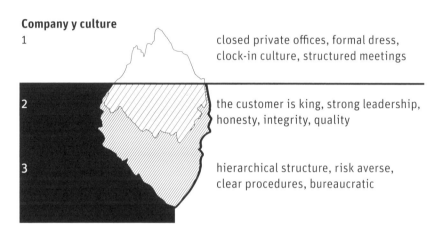

Company y culture

1 — closed private offices, formal dress, clock-in culture, structured meetings

2 — the customer is king, strong leadership, honesty, integrity, quality

3 — hierarchical structure, risk averse, clear procedures, bureaucratic

Understanding your own cultures | 1.3

In today's world, managers increasingly manage diverse groups. This diversity is created by culture – of various kinds. The variety of cultures may be complex to handle, but when managers use its potential in the right way, it is also a source of creativity and improved performance.

Culture influences the behaviour of groups of people – a group of Brazilians, a group of accountants or a group belonging to the same extended family. A culture gives group members guidance as to how to think and feel, how to act, and how to evaluate the actions of others: it is an orientation system for behaviour in the group. A culture also gives to its members a feeling of belonging and identity. It is the glue that holds the group together.

International managers firstly need to understand the various cultures of which they are members and how these cultures influence their behaviour.

Here are some international managers talking about their perceptions of their own *national* cultures. Do you see these cultures in the same way?

In France you try to enrich the meeting with imagination, new ideas and in America people are very direct, critical but never against the person, against the fact or the project. In France when you criticise a project, people think you also criticise the person.
Frédéric Thoral (France), Areva, France

In Sweden we have a 'cup of coffee' culture, which means if we have something to talk about in management we put people around the conference table with a cup of coffee. Then we talk about it.
Eric Hallberg (Sweden), TeliaSonera, Sweden

In the USA, there'd be more of a validation, "You did a good job", patting on the back a little bit.
Timothy Taylor (U.S.A.), Henkel, Germany

In Italy ….. a good feeling, good relationships are necessary for good results.
Camillo Mazzola (Italy), Henkel, Italy

People think the important thing is to have the client and take the problems later on. I was in Pakistan two weeks ago and everywhere in any kind of business they deal like this. They say "Yes we can do it". They never say no.
Sherri Warsi (Pakistan), Integrico AB, Sweden

When we have understood our own cultures and how they work, then we are ready to look at other cultures.

Profiling your own cultures | 1.4

Emotional intelligence is mainly about using insights you have about yourself to give you insight into other people. In a similar way, *cultural intelligence* is the ability to use insights you have about the *cultures you belong to* to give you insights into the *cultures of those people you interact with*.

One of the key competences of mindful international managers is awareness and understanding of their own cultural icebergs. This understanding acts as a bridge to understanding others.

Before you profile your own cultures, you need to understand the various cultures which you belong to and which impact on your behaviour.

Religious culture
Shared beliefs and norms of behaviour are part of having a certain religious faith. An outsider visiting a place where a certain religion is practised may notice that rest days are different or that people eat different food.

Socio-economic culture
Shared attitudes and lifestyles based on income and social background. Outsiders may notice that behaviour, for example consumer behaviour, is very different in one social class compared to another. Generational groups (the young, the old …) may also be seen to favour different brands and technical gadgets.

Sectoral culture
Shared experience of working in a certain sector – for example, food, pharma-ceuticals or banking. From the outside you may notice shared dress codes, and the use of shared jargon.

Functional culture
Shared experience of working in a certain function – for example, accountancy, marketing or human resources – as well as shared education and training. The onlooker may notice different attitudes to work and different priorities.

National and ethnic culture
Values and norms of behaviour shared by members of the same ethnic group or by citizens of the same nation state. In many cases, regional, tribal and linguistic sub-groups have separate cultural identities.

Organisational culture
Values and norms of behaviour shared by people working for the same organi-sation. The observer may see that processes – for example, the way meetings are organised – and communication styles are different.

 The iceberg can be used to describe any of these types of culture. What sort of culture do you think this iceberg describes?

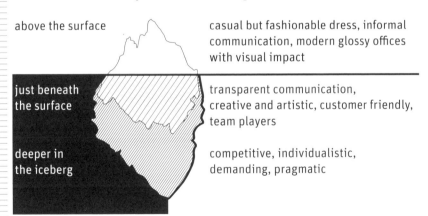

above the surface — casual but fashionable dress, informal communication, modern glossy offices with visual impact

just beneath the surface — transparent communication, creative and artistic, customer friendly, team players

deeper in the iceberg — competitive, individualistic, demanding, pragmatic

It is obvious that a person belongs to more than just one culture at a time. This can sometimes lead to conflicting preferences, for example when religious culture might suggest one behaviour and socio-economic culture another.

Which cultural groups do you feel you belong to?
Write down: (in the first column) the different cultural groups which you
belong; (in the second column) some of the values and (in the third column)
some of the behaviours of the different cultures of which you are a member.

Cultural groups	Values: beliefs and principles my culture (and I) think are important	Norms: behaviours and practices my culture (and I) prefer
My national / ethnic culture: e.g. German	e.g. honesty	e.g. direct and explicit communication
	1	
	2	
	3	
My organisational culture:	e.g. high quality	e.g. continuous improvement processes
	1	
	2	
	3	
My functional culture: e.g. advertising	e.g. imagination and creativity	e.g. tolerance for expression of unconventional ideas
	1	
	2	
	3	

Many people would say they are a member of more than the three cultures you have just been asked to think about. Consider those other types of culture described on the previous pages and profile another culture which you feel you belong to – religious, socio-economic, sectoral.

My . . . . culture:	Values: beliefs and principles	Norms: behaviours and practices
1		
2		
3		

Best practice

Focused on goals, flexible on approaches | 1.5

Effective international managers need first of all to be competent in their own environment. They need both the 'hard skills' of management (for example, organisation, financial reporting or strategic planning) and the 'soft skills' (for example, the ability to encourage and motivate their team, to focus on goals and to influence senior management). They need to reflect on their own behaviour and performance in these areas.

Key competence
Personal autonomy through focus on goals[3]

Effective international managers are goal-focused and motivated by their objectives. This is especially important because their complex working environment may distract their attention from the objectives. In spite of these difficulties they keep trying to achieve their goals. International managers may have to be more willing to adapt the approaches and methods with which they achieve their goals to local conditions.

Once they start working internationally, managers do not need to throw away all the good practice that has worked for them in their home culture. But the mindful international manager will focus not only on the outcome of his/her work but also on the process.

You need to reflect first on *your own cultural mindset* and how this influences you at work. The next chapter will look at some key areas – the way different cultures see power, time, communication and space. These underlying attitudes have a big impact on how we behave at work.

Then you need to reflect on how your international partners behave. Mindful international managers need in particular to observe how local managers work and to understand *their cultural mindset*.

Look, you need to be what you are. I am Erik and I'm Swedish and I have my own character. But at the same time when I'm setting goals I have to under-stand what is going on inside the company and the country and I try to find a melody, or tune into what works for this organisation and the specific leaders.

Erik Hallberg (Sweden), TeliaSonera, Sweden

You need to understand these differences and then perhaps adapt your good practice to the local situation, as in the saying 'When in Rome do as the Romans do'. How far and in what areas you adapt will depend on the situation you are in. You need to consider how far down the road to Rome you go! For example, if you are an expatriate working in a foreign subsidiary, you might need to adapt more and in different situations than a frequent business traveller or somebody working at home alongside foreign colleagues.

In Sweden, people can discuss openly and interactively around the table but in the Baltic States you can't do that. So you have to ask managers questions before big meetings, to get the manager on your side to share the goal.

Erik Hallberg (Sweden), TeliaSonera, Sweden

Erik realises that establishing common goals is key wherever you are. However, you need to be flexible and to adapt your approach to the culture or cultures and to the situation you are dealing with. To do this you need to take account of cultural differences. The mindful international manager is focused not only on the result but also the context and process of communication and cooperation.

Key Competence
Flexible behaviour[3]

Effective international managers display not only goal-focus but also flexibility in their behaviour. Being flexible enough to adapt to an appropriate extent is absolutely key to managing the complexity of new cultural contexts. As they are able to behave flexibly, they fit in more easily and people around them feel more comfortable.

Notes

1
For example French and Bell (1979), who attribute it to a presentation given by Stanley N. Herman in 1970. Others also use the iceberg to describe national or ethnic culture. Ruhly (1976) and Weaver and Uncapher (1981) appear to be among the first.

2
Schein (1985).

3
One of the Worldwork international competency set. Full details can be found at http://www.worldwork.biz.

Chapter 2
Difference and common ground

This chapter focuses on

the common ways in which all types
of culture tend to vary in their values
and behaviours

how values and behaviours may
vary in a person depending on
which culture is dominant in a
particular activity

how individuals may have values
and preferences which are different
from the cultures of which they are
a member

why knowledge about other cultures
is a key competence for the mindful
international manager

Competing values? |

In order to understand better the behaviours and practices you see when you work across cultures, it is necessary to explore the much larger part of the iceberg below the waterline. Here lie the values, beliefs and attitudes which underpin behaviour.

Some values are more or less universal, for example, the value of giving importance to the family and to the need to protect it. Other shared values are newer, for example, the growing sense in many parts of the world of the need to protect the planet from climate change and environmental damage. But most of our values have been formed from generations of experience within particular cultural groups.

These values guide the behaviour of members of the group. They help them to deal with the problems and opportunities which the group faces. These problems and opportunities may be similar for everyone but different groups call on different values, attitudes and behaviours for handling them.

Many cultures share some values, but the relative importance they give to these values may vary a great deal. For example, members of many cultures believe in the importance of honesty. In fact, we tend to be honest about different things and with different people.

Which options do you prefer in these situations?

1   You are rushing to an important meeting when you meet a colleague who you worked closely with up until five years ago. You have not seen her since then.

Do you stop to talk to her or do you greet her but then rush to make your meeting on time?

Here the value you place on punctuality and the task in hand could be in conflict with the value you place on relationships.

2   You arrive at the meeting and find that a key participant is not there. He arrives late and has not prepared an update as you, the project leader, requested. He says he has been very busy talking to a potential new client and decided this was more important than the update.

Do you feel he is unprofessional or flexible?

Here the value you place on planning and being prepared, plus respect for your leadership, may be in conflict with the value you place on flexibility and spontaneity.

3   Your boss keeps his distance from the team and communicates quite formally, saying it is a sign of respect for people he doesn't need to know personally. You think your boss is fair but not very approachable. You believe that communicating informally and breaking down the distance between people help to create a more productive working atmosphere.

Do you feel it would be better if your boss were more one of the team with a more informal style?

Here the value you place on showing respect may conflict with the value you place on informal relationships at work.

I met the (German) boss of the market research agency and when we shook hands to say goodbye he actually bowed. And that seemed very strange and very formal.

Market research manager (U.K.), power generation, U.K.

Power in national cultures and organisational cultures | 2.2

In some societies, hierarchy does not play as important a role as in others. Countries such as Canada and Australia, which have thrown off their colonial past, reject the need for social hierarchies.

Australians talk about the "tall poppy syndrome", a phrase used to explain the ordinary Australian's lack of respect for wealth and power. The idea is that tall poppies should expect to be cut down.

In many countries in the past there was a traditional belief that a person's social rank was fixed at birth and was unlikely to change. This belief is less strong in some parts of the world and perhaps has less hold over young people and city dwellers in some countries, although it still influences many people today. In more traditional societies, there is a belief that people should 'know their place' and not only make the best of it, but dignify their position by accepting their role. Hierarchical societies show greater deference and respect to power and authority.

Q: Is it another world again in China?

A: Yes, but as you know, French business culture is very hierarchical,

which is reassuring for the Chinese.

Frédéric Thoral (France), Areva, France

Organisational cultures show the same range of attitudes. In a large, traditional, company with many layers of organisation, managers may believe they should use the power which the company has given them. They may give orders without consulting their staff. They may think that status symbols like large company cars and big offices are normal and desirable.

On the other hand, people in a young start-up company may feel that power differences should be small. They may think that everybody should have a say in making decisions and should be encouraged to take initiatives.

There are organisational and strategic reasons why large companies may develop many-layered hierarchies. It is a way of handling increasingly complex and diverse businesses. If the national culture in which the company is located is hierarchical as well, then a top-down leadership style may become the norm. On the other hand, a younger company may believe that its entrepreneurial spirit is part of its competitive advantage. So it may want to encourage a more participative and less deferential way of behaving.

Oh, it's much more hierarchical (in our company in Germany). It's much more like in-groups – you see it in the cafeteria. There's really a separation between management and non-management. It's very strong, very strong and it's very different from the US. OK, there is a separation in terms of practicality, but in terms of one-to-one interaction, we have an underlying equality feeling. It's different in character here when you see the tables in the cafeteria, one table for management and one for non-management.

Timothy Taylor (U.S.A.), Henkel, Germany

How far do you identify with these competing values?

What's the preference of your *organisational* culture?

More hierarchy	3	2	1	0	1	2	3	Less hierarchy

What's your *personal preference* here?
Is it different from that of your organisational culture?

More hierarchy	3	2	1	0	1	2	3	Less hierarchy

Time in national cultures and organisational cultures | 2.3

People attach very different values to time in different cultures.[1]

In more time-oriented cultures, for example, in Northern Europe and North America, people tend to feel that time is finite and must not be wasted. Like money, it should be spent wisely.

Both work and play must be scheduled, and individuals must plan and prioritise. Time is so valuable that people attend time management courses in order to maximise their use of this most precious commodity.

In the Middle East, parts of Asia, Latin America and to some extent in Southern Europe, time tends not to rule your life in the same way. Many things can be done at the same time. People are not so concerned about the precise starting and stopping time of a certain activity.

Neither work nor play should be dictated by what is written in your engagement diary. In these cultures, planning and scheduling are less important since one cannot be sure what is going to happen next. You need to be flexible. You also need to respond to people and be available if they want some of your time.

In business we can see this difference in attitudes towards time clearly in meetings.

How meetings may differ across cultures

Meetings tend ...	in more time-oriented cultures	in less time-oriented cultures
to start and finish ...	on time	later than announced
to be ...	more structured	less structured
to have ...	a clear agenda which is followed	no agenda or an agenda which may not be followed
to be for ...	making decisions, agreeing actions, moving things on	other purposes as well, such as displaying the leadership competence of those in authority or cultivating relationships

Participants tend ...	in more time-oriented cultures	in less time-oriented cultures
to be expected ...	to make controlled contributions which are not too long and are to the point	to be tolerant of contributions which are off the point or of people doing other things like looking at their laptops or blackberries
to be expected ...	not to talk at the same time as others	to be tolerant of people talking at the same time as others, or talking on a mobile phone

I think it's partly a cultural thing to do with an attitude towards time. You plan and agree to meet at a certain date and time to organise work for a project, you write it down, and then the person will SMS you hours before the meeting and say "I can't come but I'll be there tomorrow" when you're not available.

Brian Cracknell (U.K.), Language Works, Malaysia

How far do you identify with these competing values?

What's the preference of your *national or ethnic* culture?

More time-oriented	3	2	1	0	1	2	3	Less time-oriented

What's your *personal preference* here?
Is it different from that of your national or ethnic culture?

More time-oriented	3	2	1	0	1	2	3	Less time-oriented

Communication in national cultures and organisational cultures | 2.4

In some cultures, for example the Netherlands or Israel, people tend to place a high value on speaking directly.[2] They feel it is important to be explicit and get to the point; they may not worry too much if they offend people on the way. They see being direct and explicit as a sign of honesty and may regard this as more important than harmonious relationships. They think that conflict will help to clear the air and allow people to move forward. They think that the important thing in conversation is to emphasise facts in order to create clarity.

> *English people like to go around the house, whereas Germans go through the front door (...) you can just be quite direct and coherent, not beat around the bush.*
> Communications manager (U.K.), power supply, U.K.

In these cultures people pay less attention to hidden messages and to information contained in the context – for example, interpreting the way their interlocutors are dressed, or their body language, or thinking about the importance of who they are related to. They pay attention to what is said. They believe that people generally say what they mean and mean what they say.

In other cultures, for example in Thailand or Saudi Arabia, people tend to place a high value on maintaining harmonious relationships with the people they communicate with, especially in public. They feel that it is important to be polite, and that this can be achieved by communicating indirectly and implicitly. They tend to be careful not to make people lose face. Conflict should be avoided or at least not confronted openly.

Business success is built more on relationships than actually what people say or promise. What is important when talking is to create common ground, to give face and to integrate everyone into a harmonious conversation.

In these cultures people pay a lot of attention to the messages implied in the context – they way you dress, the way you sit, your connections and background. They use their shared knowledge and experience to understand implied messages. The word 'no' will often be avoided. 'Yes' could mean 'I agree', 'I understand', 'I'm not sure', 'I don't know', 'I don't have the authority' or simply 'I want to be polite to you'.

> *I think for French leaders, things are implicit; we have to read between lines. For Danes and Americans things have to be explicit. And very often I am fed up about the questions because I think they do not understand me. They say to me: "But Frédéric, tell us what you want exactly."*
> Frédéric Thoral (France), Areva, France

How far do you identify with these competing values?

What's the preference of your *national or ethnic* culture?

| More direct, explicit, honesty-oriented | 3 | 2 | 1 | 0 | 1 | 2 | 3 | More indirect, implicit, harmony oriented |

What's your *personal preference* here?
Is it different from that of your national or ethnic culture?

| More direct, explicit, honesty-oriented | 3 | 2 | 1 | 0 | 1 | 2 | 3 | More indirect, implicit, harmony oriented |

However, differences between cultures are relative. For Frédéric, French managers are less direct than their Danish and U.S. colleagues. If he were working in Thailand, he would probably find most French managers more direct than most Thai managers.

In Europe, the British are often seen as polite and friendly, and less direct. As a result, it may be difficult for non-Brits (and sometimes even Brits themselves) to know where they stand. This is also because, in international business, the British are generally able to use their native language. Native speakers can often be more subtle in their use of language than non-natives.

Non-native speakers of English working together use the common language of English as a tool of communication and neither they nor native speakers of English should take offence if someone uses the language very directly.

Individualism and group-orientation in national cultures and organisational cultures | 2.5

Members of different cultures differ in how they see themselves in relation to the other members of the group.[3] In some cultures, people see themselves as essentially *independent* individuals. In other cultures, people see themselves more as *interdependent* members of a group with strong obligations to the group and its members.

In more *group-oriented* cultures,[4] such as in Japan or Malaysia, there may be more pressure to conform with group norms and to retain harmony. If your colleagues stay late at work, you tend to stay late at work. If your colleagues never disagree with their boss, you may tend never to disagree with your boss. In more *individualistic* cultures, such as in the US or the UK, it may be easier for you to behave in ways which are different from the ways your colleagues behave.

However, it is important to distinguish once again between national or ethnic cultures, organisational cultures and other types of culture. The USA may be a highly individualistic society but there are US companies which expect their employees to follow the company line and procedures very rigidly.

In individualistic national cultures, individuals are expected to look after themselves, although the support of their immediate family may be important. In a working context, this means that the focus is on the management and performance of individuals – on rewarding and promoting the most successful members of a team, for example.

It's not teamwork in the concept of the orchestra's music being greater than the individual musicians. Here, there's a lot of ownership, a lot of boundary drawing, defining your piece and taking care of it.
Timothy Taylor (U.S.A.), Henkel, Germany

In group-oriented cultures, members of the group and of the extended family are expected to look after each other. Networks play a fundamental role both at work and outside. At work, the focus is on the management and performance of the whole group or team, rewarding and celebrating group success and not picking individuals out. At home, support networks are large, consisting of extended families across generations and networks of long-standing, close friends. Friends of friends or acquaintances of acquaintances may also be expected to offer support.

It's a huge room, there are lots of people there, you have no idea what they are paid for, maybe they are close friends. There are very strong networks and you really can't understand. It's a strange and hidden network
Thomas Ruckdaschel (Germany), T-Systems, Germany about working in Jordan

Cultures do not share the same attitudes towards what is personal and private and what is public and shared. Some cultures, for example in Asia or many African countries, do not expect to protect their private lives as is done in some parts of the western world. The perfect holiday beach for an individualistic northern European may be in a quite isolated place. For other cultures, the beach is for the extended family and friends, and the more the merrier!

If you are working in Japan, you may be expected to cultivate your relations with the group by socialising with your colleagues after work. As a result, you may see little of your family in the week. Your loyalty to your colleagues and the company you work for is expected to be stronger than your loyalty to the family – at least during the week.

In German business there is no social element at all. Business in Germany is just business. It's not fun at all. It's completely different in the Arab world.
Thomas Ruckdäschel (Germany), T-Systems, Germany

In some national cultures, for example in Norway, work-life balance may be very highly valued. A common belief is that people should not let their work dominate their life, especially to the detriment of their family life.

In some countries, such as Germany, people may clearly separate different areas of their lives. There may be little or no access from working life to home life, for example. In other countries, like China or Indonesia, work and private life continually overlap.

People never seem to draw the line clearly in anything of anything.

It's quite blurred.

Li Chen (China)

How far do you identify with these competing values?
What's the preference of your *national or ethnic* culture?

| More independent | 3 | 2 | 1 | 0 | 1 | 2 | 3 | More interdependent, |
| and individualistic | | | | | | | | a group member |

What's your *personal preference* here?
Is it different from that of your national or ethnic culture?

| More independent | 3 | 2 | 1 | 0 | 1 | 2 | 3 | More interdependent, |
| and individualistic | | | | | | | | a group member |

Acquiring the kind of information presented in this chapter can mean that mindful managers better understand the differences they have to manage. Extending your knowledge of cultures is a key competence not least because it is easy to develop – through reading or talking to people who can act as cultural informants or taking part in intercultural development programmes.

Converting this knowledge into appropriate behaviour and supportive attitudes usually takes longer and may be more difficult.

Key competence
Cultural knowledge through information gathering[5]
Effective international managers are interested in finding out about cultures they are unfamiliar with. They do it through reading and observing behaviour but also by asking third parties or asking members of the cultural group themselves. They also find out more about cultures they already know and about the specific context important for their needs.

Building a common culture | 2.6

All these cultural differences could confuse and stress the international manager. Maybe this is why the inexperienced manager often says "Aren't we all the same in the end? We're all human beings". This desire to reduce the complexity in this simple way by denying that differences exist is understandable but will not lead to success.

The mindful international manager needs first to embrace the diversity – in other words, be open and curious to find out and observe the differences.

The one point is tolerance of other cultures, to appreciate the different styles.
Washington Munetsi (South Africa), Nestlé, South Africa

Having done this, you – together with your international team – need to generate a new culture and get commitment to a set of rules or guidelines which form the glue that help people to work together. These guidelines work very much like the values and norms that guide behaviour in national and ethnic cultures and organisational cultures.

My experience is that in international teams, people often are more attentive, since it seems obvious that differences exist. In national teams, people often underestimate the need for clarification. So, in some senses, international teams may be easier to manage.
Thorsten Weber (Germany), HLP, Germany

You need to clarify with your team members what values and attitudes they all share, if any, and which of them should form the common ground for the guidelines. Here are some of the questions you and your team members need to think about, bearing in mind that your answer may lie between the extremes described here. Your answer may also depend on the situation you are in.

Power
Do you believe authority and influence should be given only to the few? Do you thus attach importance to a strongly hierarchical organisation in which people know where they are and who they report to?

Or, do you believe power and influence should be shared? Do you thus value a flat, networked organisation where it is not so important what hierarchical position people hold?

Individuals and groups
Do you value being an independent individual motivated to achieve? Are you not especially interested in strong relationships with many people?

Or do you believe it more important to be a member of a larger group with its dependencies and obligations to many? For example, do you expect to mix with your colleagues socially as well as at work?

Time

Do you value time as a scarce resource to be used economically and with care? Do you therefore expect meetings to be well-prepared, punctual, and to follow an agenda and be action-oriented?

Or do you attach more importance to using time for many purposes at the same time? Do you therefore expect meetings to be less structured and more discussion and relationship-oriented?

Honesty – harmony

Do you value honesty above all else? Do you therefore expect direct and open feedback, for example?

Or do you attach great importance to harmonious relationships? Do you therefore prefer, for instance, to encourage face-to-face rather than email communication?

The rules or guidelines generated for the new common culture will thus be influenced by the cultural values and preferences of the individual team members. In this way, the guidelines need to be culture-*sensitive*.

At the same time they should be culture-*blind*: to achieve buy-in from all team members, they need to be *generated by all those in the team* rather than *imposed by the team leader or a dominant cultural majority*.

But the success of the guidelines will crucially depend on the degree of openness members of the new common culture have for something which for some may be very different from what they are accustomed to.

Key competence
Openness through acceptance[5]

Accepting behaviour and practices which are different from their own is a quality of effective international managers. They are not intolerant of different practices and do not feel threatened by them. On the contrary, they find difference interesting. They take things and people as they are.

Notes

1
Hall (1959, 1966, 1976) first drew attention to differences across cultures in concepts of time.
2
This feature was also first investigated by Hall (1976).
3
This difference was investigated by Markus and Kitayama (1991, 1994). See also Ting-Toomey (1999).
4
The difference between individualist and group-oriented cultures was investigated and brought to the attention of management by Hofstede (1980, 2001).
5
One of the Worldwork international competency set.

Individuals and groups

3

42|43

This chapter focuses on

how your actions can be influenced
by the situation you are in, the people
involved and their cultures

how cultural stereotypes can be both
useful and harmful

how effective international managers
need to take account of both culture
and personality when working in
international groups

how getting things done as a manager
depends on building relationships
with colleagues and staff

Stereotypes

When you meet a Kazak or Brazilian or German for the first time, it is all too easy to think that you now understand something about all Kazaks, Brazilians or Germans and their cultures. But in fact, a person's behaviour and actions are not solely influenced by that person's culture but result from the interplay of three factors: culture, the person involved, and the situation.

The triangle of behavioural influences

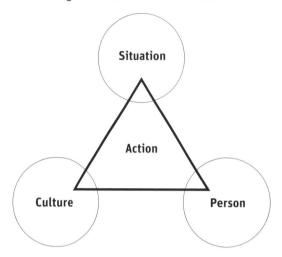

So when you meet a Slovak or a Senegalese or a Saudi for the first time, you do not necessarily learn something about the national or ethnic culture of this person. You may simply understand something about this individual's personality and preferred behaviours.

It is in fact very difficult to distinguish between what is personal and what is cultural. You need to gain much more experience of the culture in question, for example by spending a lot of time watching people from that culture working or playing together. Then it may be possible to decide whether the behaviour you see is mainly influenced by culture or by personality.

Even then, you have to be careful not to over-generalise and assume that all members of that culture are like those you have observed. What you see may be typical only of some members of it.

In building this picture of the other culture, you also have to be careful not to notice only those things which make it different from your own culture. People tend to perceive an out-group in terms of what makes it different from their own in-group. We may overlook the similarities.

It is therefore very difficult to measure the impact of culture since we are the victims of the triangle of behavioural influences. However, when you watch groups of people from the same culture, you tend to see some patterns of behaviour which repeat themselves. This is where some stereotypes come from. Other stereotypes, generally the less reliable ones, come from factors like minimal knowledge and experience, hearsay, the mass media and out-of-date school books.

Stereotypes are fixed, general images that a lot of people believe represent a particular group of people. These images may be accurate in describing what the group is like in reality. Or they may be rudimentary, incomplete and inaccurate.

These inaccurate and less reliable stereotypes can be harmful in a number of ways. In particular, they may result in us seeing only the stereotype when we encounter somebody from a different culture. We may thus ignore the individual, who may in fact be different from the stereotype.

You have to know stereotypes. For example, when I'm a German in a group, some people approach me in a certain way because they think I'm German and they expect me to act as a German. So I have to know the stereotypes, not so much to change my own behaviour, but to understand why the others behave in a certain way.

Thorsten Weber (Germany), HLP, Germany

Some researchers believe that we use stereotypes, regardless of whether they are accurate or inaccurate, to help us to make sense of the world, especially when we have little information about the situation we are in and when we have little time. They reduce the complexity of perceiving, understanding and handling new or unknown situations. For this reason – and because we often unconsciously use stereotypes in dealing with new situations – it is important that our stereotypes are based on knowledge which is accurate and up-to-date.

When stereotypes are accurate in this way and also have other features, as Nancy Adler[1] describes, the mindful manager can use them as a first best guess and a tool for managing cultural complexity. Other research makes clear why stereotypes can be harmful.

A stereotype ...

can be *helpful* as a tool for managing complexity as long as ...	can be *harmful* because it may...
you know that it is a stereotype	lead to the ignoring of individuality
it is accurate and based on sound, up-to-date and reliable knowledge	be based on very limited knowledge and experience, hearsay or the mass media
you can modify it on the basis of further knowledge and experience	influence the way we process information and what we remember
it does not evaluate the group but only describes it	fail to take account of new knowledge and experience which contradict the stereotype
you know it describes the group norm and not every member of the group	create expectations and self-fulfilling prophecies

Stereotypes are often only partly accurate because they don't describe all the members of a group. In the best of cases they may describe the norm for the group. A common stereotype could be that Dutch people communicate directly and that Thai people communicate more indirectly. But as you can see from the diagram below, some Dutch people are less direct than some Thais, even if the majority of Dutch people are much more direct.

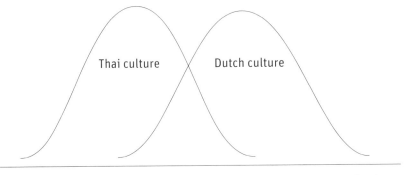

Indirect communication   Direct communication

Using stereotypes can lead you to make quick judgements about people when you first meet them. When a Canadian meets a Japanese, the experience may confirm the stereotypes they already have. The Canadian may expect to find the Japanese formal, indirect and rather reserved. The Japanese may expect to find the Canadian informal, direct and outgoing.

If we observe the Canadian and Japanese behaving in this way, the mindful international manager needs to be aware that their behaviour might be caused more by the *situation* than any cultural stereotype. For example, the Japanese is speaking English as a foreign language and this is making him seem very quiet and reserved. Or, it could relate more to *personality*. Maybe fellow-Canadians regard this Canadian as unusually outgoing.

Personality and behaviour – at work and at home | 3.2

The sociable Canadian who we met in the last section may not be so out-going when he is at home. When we are at work, we often adapt to fit with the cultural norms that we find there. When we are at home, we may show another side of ourselves.

The Johari[2] window shows us how there can be a gap between what we show and know about ourselves and what our colleagues see and know about us.

The Johari window

	Known to self	Not known to self
Known to others	**Open**	**Blind**
Not known to others	**Hidden**	**Unkown**

> The *open* quadrant is where we spend most of the time at work, displaying sides of our personality openly to our colleagues.
> Our colleagues have much less insight into how we behave at home – we may keep this side of our life *hidden* or secret.
> The *blind* spot is where our colleagues see things about us which we do not see ourselves. This could be a weakness or an opportunity – some potential to perform that we do not recognise ourselves.
> Finally, the *unknown* quadrant is the area for lying on the couch and talking about our childhood to a psychiatrist!

Personality | 3.3

Mindful international managers need to recognise that behaviour and interaction are not only influenced by *culture* – the most obvious difference from managing in their home culture – but also by *personality*. Personality and thus personal preferences have a big impact on performance because generally we do our best work when we are doing what we like. Understanding personal preferences is a good starting point for mindful international managers to get the best out of themselves and their people.

There are many psychometric tools which profile an individual's personality (e.g. Myers Briggs Type Indicator) or behaviour (e.g. Belbin's Team Role Inventory). One of them, the Team Management Profile[3] is based on four key dimensions at work:

> relationships (how we like to relate to other people)
> information (how we like to process and deal with information)
> decision-making (how we come to our decisions)
> organisation (how we organise ourselves and others)

In each case individuals can be placed on a scale:

extrovert · · · · · · · · introvert

practical · · · · · · · · creative

analytical · · · · · · · · beliefs

structured · · · · · · · · flexible

These results are then processed to give you a dominant team role located on the Team Management Wheel.

The Team Management Wheel

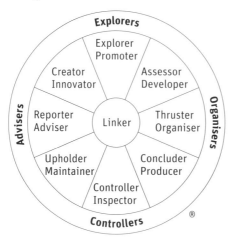

Ideally your team will consist of a balance of roles. Often this is not the case – for example, your team may have many more Explorers or Organisers and no Controllers or Advisers.

A number of factors may cause this imbalance in the team:
> a tendency for managers to recruit people like themselves
> a tendency for the industry / sector / company to favour a certain type of person
> self-selection – people choosing their job according to their personality

There is no national cultural bias evident in the more than 150,000 profiles currently held on the TMS database. In other words, for example, the proportion of introverts in Japan is not greater than in the USA. Personality type is independent of culture. However, once you are working in a group, the culture of the organisation and of the team also have a big influence on your behaviour.

Connecting personality and culture | 3.4

Relationships

Extroverts look for opportunities to meet new people. Work is a chance to network, to promote oneself and to stand out from the crowd. More *introverted* types get their energy from within themselves and are more self-motivated to achieve their tasks. They are more likely to build close relationships with a smaller number of people.

As a mindful international manager, whether you are introvert or extrovert, you need to focus on building relationships, not least because some cultures are more relationship-oriented than task-oriented. In these cultures, relationships are the key. People will do something for you (for example, deliver on time, sign a contract, make you their preferred supplier) because they like you, they feel loyalty towards you or they feel they can trust you. You cannot just rely on the quality of your products or services.

How far do you identify with these competing values?

What's the preference of your *national or ethnic culture?*

| More task-oriented | 3 | 2 | 1 | 0 | 1 | 2 | 3 | More relationship-oriented |

What's your *personal preference?*
Is it different from that of your national or ethnic culture?

| More task-oriented | 3 | 2 | 1 | 0 | 1 | 2 | 3 | More relationship-oriented |

Being open enough to build relationships with members of other cultures – maybe in contrast to your personal preferences – is another key competence of the effective international manager.

Key competence
Openness through welcoming strangers[4]

Effective international managers tend to be open to new people and to building relationships with them. They find it interesting to get to know people who are different from themselves – people with different experiences and values from their own. They are proactive in establishing relationships with others and often have a wide network of contacts.

Information

Some people are very *practical* in the way they work. They like tasks to be clear and planned. They want to know exactly what they need to do and are prepared to repeat tasks to a high level of quality. On the other hand, those who are more *creative* tend to get bored quickly, may not be so interested in detail and complexity and are prepared to work when things are not clear, or even ambiguous.

In an international work context, transparency – for example the clear definition of tasks – is very important because there is a much greater chance of misunderstanding as a result of language and distance. However, effective international management often means not understanding every-thing at once. Managers need to be able to tolerate ambiguity and deal with complexity.

Decision-making

Analytical types pride themselves on their objectivity – their ability to analyse problems and situations and work out the best decision. More *belief-oriented* people make their decisions on a more subjective and personal basis. Beliefs and principles have a greater influence on their decisions.

Analytical types will probably be more at home in cultures in which communi-cation tends to be direct and explicit and in which people spell out the factors for decision-making. Clearer boundaries and written guidelines may well be in place. On the other hand, more belief-oriented people may feel more at ease in cultures in which communication tends to be indirect and implicit and in which people avoid confrontation and maintain harmony, if at all possible.

Organisation

If you are *structured* in your work preferences, then you are probably focused on finishing tasks, keeping to deadlines, and getting on with things. A more *flexible* orientation means that you are probably less of a planner, curious and open to change, and sometimes find it difficult to finish.

To be an effective international manager, you need to be curious and open to diversity. But you also need to push ahead often in the face of difficulties and distractions to achieve your objectives. Adapting to the pace at which different cultures work may be hard if you have very structured preferences. You may easily become impatient in cultures where decisions take longer. For more flexible types, there is perhaps a chance of 'going native' – being very open to another culture but losing sight of what you are meant to achieve.

Get to know your team | 3.5

Effective international managers may need to invest more time in building relationships with the people they work with. They cannot rely only on hierarchy, position and power to exert influence and get things done.

Key competence
Influencing through rapport[4]

One aspect of influencing which is important for effective international managers consists of the ability to express warmth and attentiveness when building relationships. They make the other person feel comfortable and at ease. They are able to build personal as well as professional connections with the people they work with. This helps them to empathise with their interlocutors and to understand their perspective better. With time they are thus better able to enlist the cooperation and support of their colleagues in achieving their professional goals.

Investing time in relationships may also help you enjoy your job more.

Social relationships are vital to reach a result. So if you have everything but not the relationships, you will not obtain results. You are not in the army where you have to do it, full stop. So bad relationships can compromise a good technical job. You have to have it.

Camillo Mazola (Italy), Henkel, Italy

When you start an international project, the kick-off phase is vital. You need to allow time for the team members to get to know each other. Formal introductions are a starting point but informal socialising will be much more important in some cultures and for some individuals.

I think we are more oriented to relationships with people, no? Sometimes you have a very big problem, you go to take a coffee, you take a dinner, and you talk about everything – family, sport, and things like that.

Alejandro Pena (Mexico), Henkel, Germany, talking about working in Mexico

For people from cultures which are less relationship-oriented and more task-oriented, this phase of getting to know the team may seem a waste of time. However, if you get this step right and build on it, you will save a lot of time and misunderstandings later.

The second (important thing) would be relationships. Show a caring attitude, be genuinely interested in finding out about people and what they do, learn the language, eat the food. It's very important to share food with people to show respect.

Brian Cracknell (U.K.), Language Works, Malaysia

When you work in a domestic team, you can assume a common background and may quickly get to know and understand the personalities of the different people in the group. When you work internationally, you have to deal with the additional potential barriers of language and cultures. So you should not assume so much. If you do not restrict your assumptions, you may make some poor initial judgements of people because you cannot separate the effects of culture on behaviour from the effects of personality.

The only route to success is to invest more time in the people and be more mindful of their culturally based values and behaviours and of their individual personalities.

Best practice
The role of leadership | 3.6

The behaviour of the leader of a team, a group or a company and its declared values are the most influential factors in shaping culture.

Mindful managers in international leadership roles firstly need to know themselves. When interacting with others, they need to be mindful of their own personality, their own cultures and their leadership styles. In particular, they need to consider the leadership style which will work best in an international context.

In Sweden, if we have something to talk about in management we put people around the conference table with a cup of coffee. Then we talk about it. It doesn't work like that over there (the Baltic States). You have to find another way in line with the authoritative model which the management is using.

Erik Hallberg, (Sweden), TeliaSonera, Sweden

In a new venture, the leadership style is reinforced or rejected by success or failure. If the business or project is successful, people may assume that the leadership style was appropriate. However, it may not be the right leadership style to *sustain* success and *maintain* motivation. Expatriate managers coming into a new culture often make the mistake of believing they are in a start-up situation where they must make an impact. In fact, they are often in a 'sustain and maintain' situation, which means identifying existing success factors and reinforcing them.

You can use a SWOT analysis to understand better the existing success factors. It will also give you an opportunity to observe your new team.

SWOT analysis chart

	Helpful	Harmful
Internal (features of the team)	Strengths	Weaknesses
External (features of the environment)	Opportunities	Threats

Follow this procedure:
> Brainstorm the strengths of the team or group: what are we good at doing?
> Brainstorm the weaknesses: what are we bad at doing?
> Discuss the opportunities for success which the team can take advantage of: what can we achieve together?
> Discuss the obstacles and threats to success: what has stopped us or is going to stop us from succeeding?

Once you have completed this, identify some key actions, for example:
> Training to develop competence
> Focus on specific objectives
> Remove an obstacle

A SWOT analysis can be a key step in getting to know your team, and also in helping you to decide on an appropriate leadership style.

Notes
1
See Adler (2001).
2
Originated by Luft and Ingham (1955).
3
Developed by Margerison and McCann (1992, 1995, 1997).
4
One of the Worldwork international competency set.

Chapter 4
Direction

This chapter focuses on

how people from different cultures differ in their need for direction

how people from different cultures differ in the way they deal with uncertainty

how people in organisations can interpret vision statements differently across cultures

how intercultural influencers need a broad range of communication styles

how managers can communicate direction in different ways

The relationship between setting direction and uncertainty | 4.1

Whatever cultures you belong to, you will certainly agree that a group, a team or a company needs to know the direction it is going. Knowing the goals and methods of future action may be a universal need. What certainly varies across cultures is the importance people and cultures attach to communicating direction explicitly. The ways that are used to communicate direction appropriately and effectively may vary as well.

Germans tend to like technically clear environments. They want to know what the goals of a project are, what resources they have and so on. They need a clear plan. There are people from other countries, perhaps the UK and the US, who like to experiment. They have a framework concept and then they start and build up experience, so they work a little bit with uncertainty.

Peter Wollmann (Germany), Zurich Group, Germany

Somebody setting the direction for a group or an organisation removes uncertainty about desired future actions. Both organisational cultures and national and ethnic cultures reflect different attitudes towards uncertainty.[1] Peter Wollmann believes that the Germans feel a need to reduce and avoid uncertainty, for example, through making plans and defining procedures. They want to create certainty through having clear goals, and clear steps and processes to reach the goals.

A culture with less need for order and for avoiding uncertainty will not have the same expectations. The uncertainty of life is not viewed as a threat and therefore there is less need to plan in order to reduce and avoid uncertainty. Setting the direction can thus be less explicit.

How far does your organisation and do you identify with these competing values? Is it / are you more or less tolerant of uncertainty? Are planning and processes more or less important?

What is the preference of your *organisational* culture?

More tolerant	3	2	1	0	1	2	3	Less tolerant
Planning less								Planning more
important								important

What is your *personal preference* here?
Is it different from that of your organisational culture?

More tolerant	3	2	1	0	1	2	3	Less tolerant
Planning less								Planning more
important								important

Large organisations often try harder to avoid uncertainty as the size of the potential loss resulting from a mistake becomes higher. Smaller companies may work better with uncertainty, able to adapt to a changing environment quickly and flexibly. However, all companies want their people to know where they are going. They vary in how much direction they give and how much flexibility they permit as to how they will get there.

Direction and vision | 4.2

Organisations use vision and mission statements to communicate direction. But communicating direction in this way is a culturally sensitive matter. The vision has to make sense to the organisation's employees. People may receive vision and mission statements very sceptically if their management is not sensitive to a range of cultural preferences among its employees.

Many employees will be sceptical if management oversimplifies the vision – for example, by saying that the company wants 'to make the planet a better place'. Employees may switch off if they think the mission is arrogant – for example if the mission is 'to be number one in the global market place'. How people react depends in part on deeply-held personal and cultural preferences. The vision must be one that is compatible with these values and aspirations.

This is particularly difficult to achieve across a wide range of different national and ethnic cultures represented in an international organisation precisely because *national* culture influences these values and preferences. It may be difficult for management to achieve buy-in to a corporate value statement if it is not compatible with a very wide range of different, locally held values.

In the same way, culture also determines the meanings given to apparently universally acceptable vision statements. 'To be commercially successful' may mean increasing a company's profits, its share price, its dividend and its value to a shareholder-oriented corporation in a country such as the USA or the UK. To a small or medium-sized, family-owned and family-run company in other countries of the world, commercial success may mean being able to generate a reasonable income over the years and passing the company on to the next generation of the family.

Communicating direction:
Big picture or detail? Push or pull? | 4.3

Communicating a message about the future to a diverse group is a challenge. Some members of a team or organisation will be inspired by the ambition and vision of the big picture; others – the more pragmatic and down-to-earth types – will want to know the detail.

How do you see yourself?
Are you a big picture person or a detail person?

1 Do you skim the headlines in a newspaper getting a quick overview of the news?

2 Do you find an article and report and read it all the way through?

3 Do you get bored quickly if you have to repeat a task more than a few times?

4 Do you get satisfaction from repeating tasks to a high standard?

5 Do you like talking about ideas and concepts?

6 Do you like talking about processes and how things work?

If you are communicating direction to diverse functional groups – each with its own culture, e.g. finance, marketing, R & D, HR and production – you need to be mindful of the process. How are you going to make sense of it for such an audience? This may involve choosing between the big picture approach or the detail approach. It may involve other choices of stylistic features such as those listed below.

Profile your own preferred style of communicating by locating yourself on the scales below. Then use a different colour pen to do the same for your audience.

big picture	3	2	1	O	1	2	3	detail
formal	3	2	1	O	1	2	3	informal
distanced	3	2	1	O	1	2	3	close
conceptual	3	2	1	O	1	2	3	pragmatic
neutral	3	2	1	O	1	2	3	emotional
expansive	3	2	1	O	1	2	3	concise
optimistic	3	2	1	O	1	2	3	realistic
statements	3	2	1	O	1	2	3	questions
silent listener	3	2	1	O	1	2	3	active listener
soft arguments	3	2	1	O	1	2	3	hard facts

Pushing

This approach to communicating direction means that you communicate a strong message with good presentation skills. In a hierarchical or uncertainty-avoiding culture where expertise may be thought to be in the heads of individuals, this might be the preferred style. You need to be well-prepared and demonstrate a belief in your message.

Pulling

This means that you start by understanding the position of the people you are talking to. You may ask questions to align your message with their expectations. You allow them to interrupt and ask you questions. The communication is seen as a dialogue – to find a solution together. This approach will work well in a flatter organisational culture where there may be less belief in the power of the expert.

In both approaches, you need to be clear about your objective. The difference is how you achieve it – push or pull.

Mindful international managers realise that there isn't a single style of communicating and influencing which is appropriate and effective for all individuals and all cultures. What is more, they are able to select an approach from a range of styles which best suits the people and cultures in question. The style they choose may be more similar to that of their audience or the person they are talking to.

Key competence
Influencing by using a range of communication styles[2]

One aspect of influencing which is important for effective international managers is the ability to select from a range of styles an approach which best suits the situation, the people and the cultures in question. They are able to analyse their interlocutors' preferred communication style and tune into their wavelengths. They can thus use a style which their interlocutor feels comfortable with. They have a broad repertoire of communication styles with the result that they can communicate effectively and appropriately with people from different cultures and backgrounds.

Long and short term orientation | 4.4

In communicating direction, is it more appropriate to emphasise the long-term or the short term? It is a common belief that US companies tend to focus on short-term profit – bottom-line results – and that Japanese companies may focus more on long-term return on investment in order to achieve market position. Regardless of whether this stereotype is accurate or not, it identifies an important cultural preference,[3] which you may need to consider when communicating direction in international business.

The profound person understands what is moral.
The small person understands what is profitable (Confucius).

Confucius felt that li

(profit, gain, advantage) was not a proper motive for actions affecting others.

A different attitude towards virtue underlies the long- or the short-term orientation. In long-term oriented cultures, the virtues which are valued and promoted are those which are geared towards future rewards, especially the value of trying hard to achieve goals, even in the face of difficulty; and the value of being careful with money.

In cultures with a shorter-term orientation, virtues are promoted which relate more to the present. Money is not saved but spent. Concrete results are looked for quickly. Having made the profit, the investors expect the return. In a longer-term culture, people are willing to wait longer for good results and are less impatient to take their return.

How do you see your culture at work? Choose the statement which more closely corresponds to your view.

1   a. We value colleagues who are persistent and patient. (0)
    b. We value colleagues who are dynamic and focused on results. (1)

2   a. We value people who have acquired their status and reputation over a long period of time. (0)
    b. We value people who have risen quickly and reached their position at a young age. (1)

3   a. We value personal time for life outside work. (1)
    b. We do not value personal time. (0)

4   a. We tend to save and be thrifty. (0)
    b. We tend to spend and acquire goods. (1)

5   a. We tend to make long-term investments (e.g. in property). (O)
     b. We tend to make short-term investments
     (e.g. in money or on stock markets). (1)

6   a. We focus on market position for long-term returns. (O)
     b. We focus on short-term results. (1)

7   a. We believe that we can identify clearly what is right and wrong. (1)
     b. We believe that right and wrong is rarely black and white. (O)

Scoring: the higher your score, the more you see your culture at
work as short-term oriented.

Past, present and future | 4.5

The mindful international manager also needs to be aware that cultures may
differ in the value they attach to the past, the present and the future.[4] This
different emphasis may have effects on how managers give direction and how
a multicultural team or workforce regard direction once it has been given.

Past orientation
In some cultures people believe everything can be found in the past. Life
repeats itself so we can learn from the past how to deal with the present and
the future. This means we need to see the direction that other people took in
the past and learn from them. Cultures which stay close to their traditions and
rituals place high importance on knowing and understanding the past. In
addition, older people are highly respected because they know more about
the past than the young.

Present orientation
Some cultures and groups, for example many sports teams, are much more
present-oriented. They believe that success comes from focusing on the
moment, not dwelling on past successes or failures or dreaming about future
achievements. Countries suffering ongoing difficulties, such as war or
deprivation, can also be more present-oriented than, for example, more
fortunate countries. They may believe that it is not worth spending too long
planning and predicting, as the key to survival is in the present.

Future orientation
A culture which focuses on the future needs to be optimistic. There is a belief
that anything is possible with the right planning and resources. Future-
oriented cultures do not believe in dwelling too much on the past. People
believe you need to have a vision and sense of purpose to get the best out
of your future.

How would you represent your national or ethnic culture?

Use circles to illustrate your culture's time orientation. Think of the past, present and future as being in the shape of circles. In the space below draw three circles, each representing either the past, the present or the future. Use different sized circles to represent their relative importance. Arrange these circles in the way that best shows how your culture tends to feel about the relationship of the past, present and the future. If the circles you draw intersect, you see a connection between the various periods. If they are separate, you see no connection.[5]

The three circles below would indicate that the past is very important in comparison with the present and that the future is relatively speaking less important. All three periods are unconnected with each other.

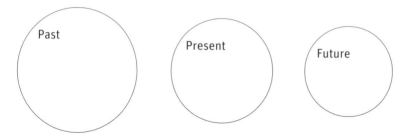

The next three circles show how the three periods are regarded as equally significant and how the present is influenced equally by the past and future.

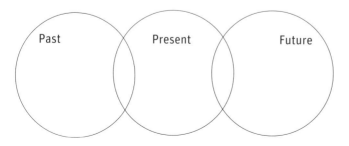

Top-down or bottom-up or something else? | 4.6

How involved do you want your team to be in setting the direction? Is strategy the preserve of senior management or can others contribute to defining the direction and the objectives?

Top-down communication

In chapter 2 we saw how some cultures are more hierarchical than others. In these more hierarchical organisational cultures, there is often an expectation that top management should set the direction. Seniority gives leaders authority and encourages a willingness to obey and follow.

> *The Malays still have almost a feudal attitude to power. The man who is at the top gets our support because he is at the top. Whether he's wrong doesn't come into it. We must follow him.*
> Brian Cracknell (U.K.), Language Works, Malaysia

Bottom-up communication

In less hierarchical national and organisational cultures, you need to make sure that you don't 'talk down' to your colleagues, especially if you are their boss. In these cultures, the process of gaining consensus is vital for getting commitment – achieving buy-in – to a common goal.

> *In Scandinavian countries it is no problem that a direct report of the CEO becomes his project leader, whereas in African countries where I have been working recently, this is impossible.*
> Thorsten Weber (Germany), HLP, Germany

It is not always a question of hierarchy. In very structured and formal organisations or in cultures with a strong need to avoid uncertainty, everybody has a role and contributes only within their specific field of expertise.

> *The feeling here is that you are responsible for bringing in your piece. It must be done. You should answer the questions you have to answer. But it's not the kind of cooperative working and learning we have more in the US.*
> Timothy Taylor (USA), Henkel, Germany

Communicating direction to a team is vital. International managers need to get their international teams all moving in the same direction but, from the intercultural perspective, the mindful manager needs to be flexible about how to do this.

Communicating direction

Techniques	Advantages	Disadvantages
Top-down		
The leader decides and then communicates direction.	Can be inspiring if you have a broad enough range of influencing skills.	Less suitable for less hierarchical cultures.
Bottom-up		
The leader listens to the ideas and anxieties of the team's members before s/he and the team reach a consensus about direction.	Can create new alternatives and synergies.	May become a talking shop if you don't drive things forward. Less suitable for more hierarchical cultures.
Talk to individuals		
Giving direction on a one-to-one basis.	Each team member gets understanding of direction and may buy in to it. May be a useful addition in individualistic cultures.	Does not develop team spirit.
Talk to team		
Giving direction to the whole group.	Can be inspiring if you have a broad enough range of influencing skills.	May fail to gain buy-in from some individuals who the manager does not notice.
Big picture		
The leader stresses major goals and opportunities.	May achieve a broad commitment. May be more suitable in cultures tolerant of uncertainty.	May fail to convince pragmatic team members who may dismiss it as a public relations exercise and not take it seriously.
Details		
The leader presents goals and perhaps also methods in detail.	Will appeal to the practical team members. May be more suitable in cultures with a high need for certainty.	Leads to reflection about specific individual roles and not enough about the team as a whole.

In many cases, the answer is to balance a top-down with a bottom-up approach. Effective international managers need to have clear sense of where they want to go. But then they need to involve their teams in implementing this direction and adapting it to the particular needs of the situation. In this way, they may not only be creating something new in the culture of their organisation or part of the organisation. They will also be building on the cultural diversity of the group.

I usually started by saying that this is our goal, now let's sit together and see how we can adapt it to fit you and your country in your company. So it was a common process as much as possible.

Birgitta Gregor (Germany), HLP, Germany

Notes

1
This insight was brought to intercultural management by Hofstede (1980, 2001).

2
One of the Worldwork international competency set.

3
This insight goes back to work by Chinese Culture Connection (1987) and was then also reported on in Hofstede (1994) and Hofstede (2001).

4
This is an insight developed by the anthropologists by Kluckhohn and Strodtbeck (1961) and made famous in the international management world by Trompenaars (1993).

5
This exercise is a variation of the Cottle Circle Test published in Cottle (1967). Cottle's original version was brought to international management by Trompenaars (1993).

Chapter 5

Organisation and change

This chapter focuses on

what values and attitudes may hinder or support the management of change in international business

the consequences of organisational change

working in international projects as a driver of organisational change

how people working internationally must sometimes adapt to working without a leader

how communication is of critical importance to managing change successfully

Attitudes towards change | ^{5.1}

International management operates in a constantly changing environment, which makes it imperative for international organisations to be able to change quickly too. Managing such change is a frequent task of international managers. The mindful international manager must therefore understand what are the *drivers* of change in cultures and in people, and what are the *blockers* of change.

A framework of values[1] developed by Shalom Schwartz contains a key set of values called 'conservation'. People who think these values are important may find it difficult to accept change.

Possible blockers of change
How far is the person described like you?

Conservation values

Conformity
Does what he/she is told, follows the rules, behaves properly, shows respect to his/her elders, is obedient, is polite, does not disturb others

very little   1   2   3   4   5   6   7   very much

Security
Avoids danger, is organised and tidy, finds social stability important

very little   1   2   3   4   5   6   7   very much

Tradition
Is satisfied with what he/she has, finds religion and customs important, does things the traditional way, is modest

very little   1   2   3   4   5   6   7   very much

Adapted from the Portrait Values Questionnaire[2] developed by Shalom Schwartz.

People who think that these conservation values are important want to know where they stand. They tend to prefer the established order. To get buy-in for change from people with these values, the effective international manager needs to communicate about changes in the organisation very clearly:

> Organisation and roles. You need to state clearly who will report to whom and what they will be responsible for.
> Processes and systems. You need to state clearly and step by step how new processes will work.

You have to adapt to people who need to refer to what has been said and what has been agreed and planned. If some are very creative and loose, then you can do it in another way, more relaxed and informal.

Lorenzo Pestalozzi (Switzerland), CRPM, Switzerland

On the other hand, the international manager could be working with people for whom a different value set in the Schwartz framework is more important. This set is called 'openness to change'.

Possible drivers of change
How far is the person described like you?

Openness to change values

Hedonism
Seeks fun and pleasure, wants to enjoy life

very little   1   2   3   4   5   6   7   very much

Stimulation
Does lots of different things, seeks new activities, likes surprises and excitement

very little   1   2   3   4   5   6   7   very much

Self-direction
Is creative and imaginative, likes freedom to decide, plans and chooses, is curious, wants to understand many things, likes to be independent and self-reliant

very little   1   2   3   4   5   6   7   very much

Adapted from the Portrait Values Questionnaire[2] developed by Shalom Schwartz.

People who score high on this scale are more likely to be open to change than people who score high on the conservation set of values. In fact, they may well get bored without some change. The mindful international manager needs to keep them involved by giving them opportunities to do new and different things and to give them freedom in their work so that they can enjoy themselves.

Key competence
Spirit of adventure[3]
Effective international managers are emotionally strong and have a sense of adventure. They look for variety, change and stimulation in life and avoid what is safe and predictable. They put themselves into uncomfortable, ambiguous and therefore demanding situations. But they know they can learn from the experience.

Changing organisational structure |

To remain agile in a fast-moving business environment and also to reduce costs, many organisations have reduced the number of layers that they have. This is not just a structural change. It needs to be supported by cultural change. Both types of change demand flexibility from the mindful international manager. Mindful international managers need to be aware of the possible deep-seated blockers to this kind of change in themselves and in their staff and their colleagues.

The cultural iceberg for a many-layered organisation could look like this:

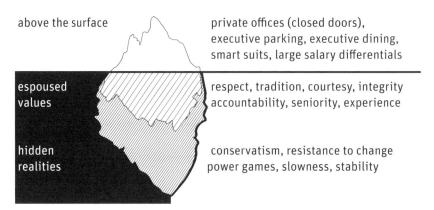

above the surface	private offices (closed doors), executive parking, executive dining, smart suits, large salary differentials
espoused values	respect, tradition, courtesy, integrity accountability, seniority, experience
hidden realities	conservatism, resistance to change power games, slowness, stability

For Germans, if there is a hierarchy, there is a push to work in that team because the authority has more influence in German guys. In Latin guys, hierarchical pressure is less important so you must have more and more charismatic leadership because the hierarchy is not enough. In Germany I saw teams producing good results even if there was a very bad feeling among the team members. People execute orders even if they are not happy.

Camillo Mazzola (Italy), Henkel, Germany

The cultural iceberg for a flat organisation could look like this:

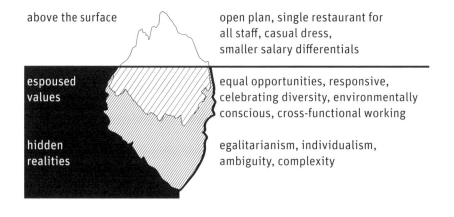

above the surface	open plan, single restaurant for all staff, casual dress, smaller salary differentials
espoused values	equal opportunities, responsive, celebrating diversity, environmentally conscious, cross-functional working
hidden realities	egalitarianism, individualism, ambiguity, complexity

Making the cultural transition to an organisation with fewer layers takes time. In particular, managers need to address the issue of motivation in a way which is sensitive to the values of their people. For example, in a delayered organisation there are fewer promotion opportunities: there are fewer rungs on the career ladder so you may have to wait longer to move up. So it may be necessary for managers to try to create other opportunities for the development of their people, which are clear and well supported. If they do not, staff turnover may well increase.

Working in international projects as a driver of organisational change | 5.3

Projects are one of the main instruments of implementing and managing change in organisations. Project leaders need to take account of attitudes to change when they select the team members (if they can) and when they set up their own project organisation. Project leaders are often not the hierarchical boss of their project team members. Each project member will usually have a line manager to whom they report.

This 'transversal' context is more complex when working internationally. Project members may be working in a quite different national or ethnic environment in their line functions. Often they will also come from different professional or functional cultures and maybe even from different organisational cultures. Notice how the innovation project team below brings together different hierarchical levels, functions and countries.

Innovation project

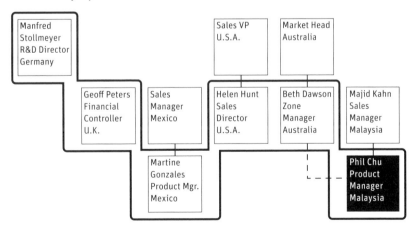

DPI Story © York Associates 2007

Phil Chu, product manager from Malaysia describes his situation like this:

"I am a product manager working in the main office in Kuala Lumpur, I report to Majid Khan, sales manager for pet food category. He's fair but a very demanding boss. This business is growing rapidly and I am responsible for a key category – premium dog food. We have very ambitious targets and my own remuneration package is linked to achieving these targets. I'm really pleased to be working on this international project but it is going to be difficult to find the time. I already notice that the other people in the project are quite direct and also demanding!"

Effective project leaders need to make sure all project members understand the local roles. It is important you spend time exploring the organisational and cultural background of each project member:

> Organisation: e.g. reporting structure, main performance measures, leadership style
> Culture: e.g. key dimensions such as power, time, communication

A common cause of tension in international projects is that they are usually initiated and driven by head office and often locally resisted because people don't like the idea of 'head office imperialism'! Mindful international project managers have to work even harder to show that they understand local cultures and also to explain their own cultural context and expectations.

It was partly due to the business environment of a German company having acquired a US company. Maybe if it had been the other way around, the situation would have been totally different. And in the finance team we had more challenges than other teams, maybe because of the functional culture – we had more rules than others which we had to follow and implement.

Wibke Kuhnert (Germany), Henkel, Germany, talking about an international project

Working without a leader as a feature of organisational change | 5.4

One result of working in international projects, and also virtually, is that your project leader is often not present. For individual team members this may in itself be a change and therefore needs the careful attention of both the project leader and the individual members. The project leader has to build a strong organisation and project culture which does not need micro-managing. The two keys to this are *transparency*, and *autonomy and support*.

Transparency

The team leader needs to organise and explain clearly scheduling, task allocation, reporting and communication within the project group. For example, some people may feel frustrated when a team member does not respond to an email within 24 hours or whatever period has been agreed. People can feel pressurised by unexpected demands (for example, a change of deadline without any discussion or warning). Rules and guidelines need to be generated and agreed during the kick-off.

> *Then, in the kick off, to give a short background, objectives, why this team and not another team, critical issues, responsibilities, reporting, allocation of tasks, who does what … and, especially, next steps.*
> Camillo Mazzola (Italy), Henkel, Germany

Autonomy and support

Project members need to be self-motivated. They may not get much support day to day. They need to be able to work on their own and keep to deadlines without being chased. This means that choosing team members who also have the right set of intercultural competences is critical – but not always practicable:

> *For an important team, you have to spend a lot of time choosing the right guys. Sometimes this decision is taken very rapidly without consideration of the impact on the future. And because we sometimes don't have the time available, it happens that the best guys are not always chosen but the guys who have more time available.*
> Camillo Mazzola (Italy), Henkel, Germany

The effective team leader needs to think about how team members are going to be supported during the life of the project. Sometimes the answer is to set up some peer or external coaching or mentoring or both.

> *Q: How open are organisations to using coaching as a form of support?*
> *A: What we see is that it depends on the mindset whether the companies consider external help as weakness or as a professional strength for achieving a better performance.*
> Frank Kuehn (Germany), HLP, Germany

Certainly the project leader needs to keep in touch with all his team members and regularly check on their current thoughts and feelings about the project. When you are working face-to-face, it is sometimes clear from facial expressions and body language how people feel. If you are working virtually, you need to work a lot harder at understanding the mood of your team members.

The four Ps | 5.5

Effective international managers follow the four Ps to make sure their teams are well-organised.

Preparation

Because your colleagues work in different contexts, it is very important to prepare for your cooperation. Before a meeting, you need to define the timing, the agenda, the documentation and the contributions you expect people to make during the meeting. Before a telephone call, send an email to agree the timing and purpose of the call.

People working in cultures which value certainty (see chapter 4) and try to avoid uncertainty may well interpret signs of thorough preparation as an indication of good management. However, people working in cultures which place less importance on certainty may have a different view of this management style.

Purpose

Make sure that everybody understands the reason why you are doing something. Do not just assume they will understand it. For example, it may be that working in your own culture, you always start a meeting with an update from all the participants. In other cultures, they may do this before in writing. You need to explain why you want to include this step at the beginning of the meeting.

When you start a telephone call, clearly state the purpose – what you hope to get out the call: "I'm calling about the shipment. I'd like to clarify the dates." It may be necessary to make your needs and intentions clear to an extent that is not necessary in your own culture in order to help create trust. This ability is a key competence of the mindful international manager.

Key competence
Transparency through exposing intentions[3]
Effective international managers make clear what their needs and intentions are – they say not only what they want but why and how. They make key messages explicit. They don't concentrate only on the foreground but fill in the background too. This helps to build up trust.

Process

Make sure that everybody understands how you want to work. Go through the steps, especially your expectations for actions and follow-up. Many meetings fail because it is not clear to the participants how to follow up. They may misunderstand the urgency or importance of a follow-up action.

But be open and flexible enough to accommodate the wishes and needs of your team members where possible. The mindful international manager recognises these needs and is able to balance a focus on goals with openness and flexibility.

People

Always remember that organisation means organising people. They are not just material resources. They may be anxious about a new process or they may feel that they have not been involved. Get feedback from them and tune in to their feelings about the project or their part of it.

Naturally being more on the Latin part, I constantly use planning methods and tools to control my spontaneous and creative side. I let it roll free or imprison it a bit, depending on the activity. If it's for developing business in an unknown environment, finding new markets, then I let my creativity loose, and just fit loose guidelines. If the environment is more local or more basic management topics, then I plan and structure more what I do.

Lorenzo Pestalozzi (Switzerland), CRPM, Switzerland

Notes

1
See for example Schwartz (1992, 1994, 1999) and Schwartz and Bardi (2001).

2
The Portrait Values Questionnaire, developed by Shalom Schwartz, is first reported on in Schwartz et al (2001). An earlier version (The Portraits Questionnaire) is reported on in Schwartz, Lehmann and Roccas (1999). These questionnaires are reproduced in part or in full in various internet and print publications, for example in Burgess and Steenkamp (1999), Schwartz et al (2001) and Davidov (2008).

3
One of the Worldwork international competency set.

Chapter 6
Roles

Managing across cultures is crucially influenced by the differing perceptions and beliefs about the roles a manager has to play, about what people expect a manager to be and do. A manager can wear many hats. Some hats are favoured more in some cultures than in others.

Many managers have a largely operational role, working without much administrative support: they may spend a lot of their time organising and administering. Other managers have a 'hands-off' role, delegating most of the work, and working at a distance from their teams so that they can think and act more strategically. The manager as coach is a relatively new role. In this role, managers support and develop their staff.

Ideally, when you are a leader and you give a clear direction, the team understands that this is the right direction. And that takes some time because you need the commitment and so on. Sometimes to save time you push the team before you have the commitment. Sometimes you can't do the perfect job. You have to do the job.

Camillo Mazzola (Italy), Henkel, Italy

Ken Blanchard and Paul Hersey in their situational leadership model[1] describe leadership style in terms of the amount of *direction* and *support* that leaders give to their staff.

Directive behaviour relates first and foremost to the task to be done. Highly directive behaviour consists in the leader telling people what to do and how, and when and where to do it. The highly directive leader sets goals, organises, directs and controls.

Supportive behaviour relates more to the relationship between leaders and their reports and the nature of their interaction. Highly supportive behaviour consists in the leader engaging in two-way communication with their people, listening actively, and facilitating interaction. The highly supportive leader gives emotional support and provides feedback.

The grid on the next page contrasts the supportive and directive styles of management. It defines four styles of management and describes the kind of staff each style is suited to.[2]

	Low ⟶ Directive behaviour ⟶ High

<table>
<tr>
<td rowspan="2">↑ High

Supportive behaviour

Low ↓</td>
<td>

Supporting leaders ...
> facilitate their people's efforts
> encourage
> participate
> share responsibility for
  taking decisions

*Appropriate for managing
staff with moderate to high
competence but who lack
confidence or motivation*

</td>
<td>

Coaching leaders ...
> explain
> ask for suggestions and ideas
> support progress
> sell and persuade
> take decisions with dialogue
  and explanation
> direct and monitor closely

*Appropriate for managing staff
with some competence but less
confidence and commitment*

</td>
</tr>
<tr>
<td>

Delegating leaders ...
> give responsibility for
  taking decisions and solving
  problems to their people
> observe
> monitor

*Appropriate for managing
staff with high competence and
high commitment*

</td>
<td>

Directing leaders ...
> tell
> guide
> monitor task
  accomplishment closely
> take decisions and pass
  them on

*Appropriate for managing
staff with less competence but
high commitment*

</td>
</tr>
</table>

	Directive behaviour	
Low		High

Adapted from Blanchard, Zigarmi and Zigarmi (1985), Hersey (1985)
and Hersey, Blanchard, and Johnson (2001)

▬ **Profile:**
your own preferred style of management,

the preferred management style of the organisation you work in

the type of staff you are dealing with.

More and more managers have both a local and an international role.
These roles may conflict with each other. Typically, pay and incentives are
decided locally. Performance measurement and support are also often a local
responsibility. The manager may well have a demanding line manager locally
who pushes for resources and results. On the other hand, the local manager
may have to take part in international projects which are important to the
company's global success. These projects are usually initiated by head office
and local companies may quite often resist them.

For international projects, you often have problems coming up
between headquarters and subsidiary.
Birgitta Gregor (Germany), HLP, Germany

Headquarters may see its task as exploiting the size of the organisation,
spreading best practice across the company and maximising global results.
The task of local subsidiaries is usually to maximise market share, sales and
profitability in their market.

Mindful international managers, whether they work in head office or in a local
subsidiary, need to understand both contexts and the causes of resentment
and conflict that such conflicting tasks may mean for the individual manager
working internationally.

Q: You worked in the US and experienced some conflict there.
What were the causes?
A: It was partly due to the business environment of a German company having
acquired a US company. Maybe if it had been the other way around, the situa-
tion would have been totally different. And in the finance team we had more
challenges than other teams, maybe because of the functional culture – we had
more rules than others which we had to follow and implement.
Wibke Kuhnert (Germany), Henkel, Germany

Once you have understood why there is resistance, you need to identify some
common goals which will unite local and international teams. The obstacle to
overcome is often that local staff do not buy into the international objectives:
they are not an incentive or motivation for them. In this case, you can review
roles, so that you understand better what is needed locally and what you can
realistically expect internationally.

Finding the fine line between having clear role definitions and fluidity and
flexibility, this is the art of project and team management.
Torsten Weber (Germany), HLP, Germany

The role of the expert and the role of the manager | 6.3

In many cultures, managers are firstly experts in their chosen field – for example mechanical engineering, accountancy or law – and only secondly managers. Organisations recruit such managers because of their qualifications and experience in a specialised area. They then promote them because they have shown themselves to be very competent in this 'technical' field. They may, however, end up in a management position that allows them very little time to be an expert, because they are now fully occupied with managing people.

This concept of the manager as an expert may also shape the expectations of a manager's staff.

▰ For example, do you agree with this statement?
"It is important for a manager to have at hand precise answers to most of the questions that subordinates may raise about their work."

This bar chart shows the percentage of managers asked who agreed with André Laurent's[3] question:

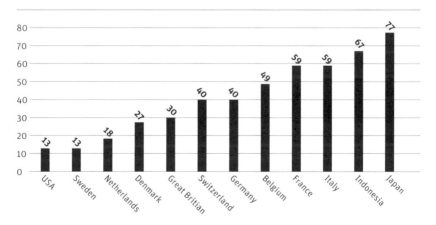

Adapted from Laurent 1986: 94

In some cultures, this belief in expert knowledge is very strong. It is connected with the culturally based preference for avoiding uncertainty and creating certainty which we saw in Chapter 4. Knowing a lot about something may allow some cultures to handle the uncertainty of the future better. People believe that their expert knowledge equips them to deal with a wider range of future possibilities.

Signs of this are visible to all. For example, the high status given to professional qualifications and to titles indicating expert knowledge and competence rather than hierarchical position shows that the culture values expertise highly. When working in such a culture, you may not be expected to contribute in an area outside your field.

Some (people) very clearly were thinking "Why are you saying this? This is not your territory." The feeling here is that you are responsible for bringing in your piece, it must be done. You should answer the questions you have to answer.

Timothy Taylor (USA), Henkel, Germany

In some cultures, there is a stronger generalist tradition in education. In these cultures, qualifications may have a smaller role to play and experience is valued instead. People may see a qualification in an arts subject – history or philosophy, for example – as a sign of a good general education which has developed sound analytical and presentational skills. They believe that training on the job will fill the gap in specialist knowledge.

The value attached in a particular culture to the subject of a qualification also varies across cultures. In many cultures, both in the developed and developing world, professions such as law and medicine are highly prized. In the USA, a law degree is a common qualification for the business world. There are said to be more lawyers per head of population in the USA than anywhere else in the world. France and Germany have a long tradition of educating good engineers and qualifications in engineering have a high status. In the UK, engineers have lower status and are less well paid.

Profile your culture's attitudes towards expert knowledge by considering these questions:

1 What types of qualification are most highly valued?

2 Who tends to get to the top of companies – sales, financial, legal people … ?

3 How easy is it to move from one field of professional expertise to another – for example to make a switch from a technical field into a commercial field?

4 Is it important to put titles and letters before (e.g. Dr or Dipl Ing) or after your name (e.g. BA Hons) on your business card?

5 Are business qualifications (for example MBAs) becoming a necessary qualification to progress up the management ladder?

The role of the influencer | 6.4

Influencing people by convincing them and persuading them is a key activity of the successful international manager. Managers by themselves can achieve surprisingly little. They are dependent on others to support them. They need to get the support of their colleagues, their staff and their own managers and influence them so that they contribute to the goals that the organisation has set.

This influence can be exerted in a number of ways. In cultures with a strong need to avoid uncertainty (see above) managers can often use *expert knowledge* and *objective facts and argument* to convince people that a particular course of action is the right one.

Influencing through networks

In other, perhaps more relationship-oriented cultures, international managers can use different *networks of relationships* to exert influence. This occurs on the basis of the rights and obligations which result from knowing somebody personally or being put in touch with somebody through the network.

Many companies have reduced the number of levels in their structure to create flatter and more *networked organisations*, which themselves are linked to other organisations by different sorts of networks. Such networks function not least through the relationships of managers with other managers.

However, these networks are created not merely by good relationships but sometimes build on *existing networks of relationships*. One of the very difficult things to understand when working in a new culture is the basis of the networks which tie people together.

Some networks may have a particularly high status in a culture. International managers need to be able to recognise high status groups as they will have particular influence in a culture. The network may be based on different types of cultural grouping. For example:

> Tribe. In tribal cultures, as can be found in many parts of Africa, membership of a certain tribe is often crucial to success.
> Education. In some cultures, an 'old school network', based on having attended a certain school or university.
> Age. Both extremes can be found. In some cultures, older, more experienced people form the elite network. In others, youth is the important entry card.
> Family. In cultures where the extended family is the main social unit (for example, in many Asian and South American countries), key networks may well be based on these extended families.

Another type of network is described by the concept of *guanxi*. At the heart of Chinese society, guanxi is a network of friends and acquaintances who feel they have obligations to support one another. They will ask for favours from those with whom they have guanxi. In this way, a network of good contacts in China can help you achieve things which are otherwise impossible to achieve. Having good guanxi is a powerful instrument for getting things done.

The mindful international manager has to take care to understand how these networks work in each new culture.

First of all, even after a few weeks here, I am still observing how people approach things, how they expect things from you.

Luis Ortega (Spain), Henkel, Germany, talking about working in Turkey

Influencing through people with influence

Power plays an important part in all business. You need to understand who has power – who is the right person to influence.

It's very challenging actually to identify who has influence in the room, who is advising the boss. It's not obvious. Everybody looks equal but they are not. In this group there are one or two who give the boss very strong advice and you can be sure he listens to them.

Thomas Ruckdäschel (Germany), T-Systems, Germany, talking about working in the Middle East

Mindful international managers are aware that influence in an organisation cannot only be achieved by doing a good job and hoping this will bring the influence they want. They are sensitive to where 'political' power lies – especially in relationship-oriented and in hierarchical cultures. They learn how to identify who the key influencers are.

The person with influence and the power to decide is often protected by informal 'gate-keepers' – personal assistants and other staff who do not themselves have the power to decide. However, a key way to reach the person with power is to build relationships with these staff. They will open doors for you if they like and respect you. If you are used to working in a very task-oriented culture, this may be difficult to adapt to. Maybe you feel you should be able to talk to the person who can get things done. However, in cultures which place greater emphasis on relationships, you may only be listened to if you are liked or trusted.

Key competence
Influencing through sensitivity to context[4]

Effective international managers understand where 'political' power lies in companies. They give time and energy to identifying who holds this power and how to get access to them.
They understand the contexts in which decisions are made and how to influence decision-makers in order to exert the influence they are aiming at.

The role of the connecter |

Bringing people together across all kinds of cultures – acting as a connecter – is a key role of international managers. In this role, they can help to break down the silo mentality.

Silo mentality

In organisational cultures, the silo mentality grows as a result of over-structuring the organisation, which may amount to putting people into boxes. These boxes, or departments, can become highly effective centres of expertise. But they may equally well turn into little kingdoms which their heads jealously guard and which are insulated from positive outside influences.

In national cultures, this closed mentality can be seen when we compare majority and minority cultures. A majority culture is one which dominates or is very powerful globally. The United States has been the world's main majority culture for the last sixty years. In the nineteenth century, Britain and France with their extensive empires, were majority cultures. A majority culture tends to look inward and to find many of the answers it needs within its own culture. It may assume that the outside world wants to imitate its own culture.

In Europe, a Scandinavian country such as Norway is a good example of a minority culture. People living in minority cultures tend to look outwards for trade, jobs, education and other things. As a result, the culture is more outward-looking and open to the influence of other cultures.

International managers need to build a strong working culture with shared values and expectations. However, they need to make sure at the same time that this culture is open and curious about other cultures. This can start with international managers themselves being open to new ideas, behaviours and people from different cultures.

Key competence
Openness through new thinking[4]
Being receptive to ideas which are different from those common
in their own culture is a quality of effective international managers. They are curious and try to extend their understanding of
different professional areas, different organisations and different
cultures. They put themselves in the position of people who are
very different from themselves and they try to see things from
other people's standpoints.

From a functional point of view, this aim of creating openness means building
cross-functional teams and networks. The manager needs to take on the role
of the connecter. Managers need to take every opportunity to bring functions
together. For example, training courses can provide a chance for people from
technical fields to develop more understanding of their colleagues in the
commercial area, and vice versa.

Knowledge transfer sessions can be built into weekly or monthly team
meetings so that expertise in a particular area does not remain just in the
heads of certain individuals. Other communication channels can be used such
as annual workshops, newsletters and video-conferences to build stronger
cross-functional networks. Connecting can go even further. Cultures which
value expert knowledge less may enable people to move across functions in
their career – for example from production into marketing.

Best practice
Defining roles | 6.6

Role definition and expectations are critical both inside and outside a team.
International managers will probably need to fulfil a wider range of roles than
at home. Depending on the cultures with which they are working and the tasks
they are performing, they may well need to be able to reflect upon what role is
most critical and flexibly adapt to the requirements of the situation.

In international projects, you are not usually able to observe team members
perform their work. You only see the results of their work. So everybody in
the team needs a clear understanding of what is expected of him or her.
This is also critical to how the team is seen from outside, especially by local
management. Team members need to know what the role involves and why it
is important. Otherwise, they will soon think it is not as important as their
local work.

Defining roles in an international team

Activity	Questions to be answered
Communicating	Who do you communicate with and how?
Managing information	What information do you need? What information do you produce and who else needs it?
Monitoring and reporting	Whose work do you monitor? Who monitors your work? When and how?
Decision-making	What do you decide? Who else decides what else?
Budgeting and controlling	Who has budget responsibility?
Producing things	What are the project targets and milestones? What responsibilities for targets and milestones do you have? Who has overall responsibility for targets?
Creating and developing things	How innovative are you expected to be and in what areas?
Assuring quality	How is it measured and by whom?
Developing yourself and others	How can this be done? What opportunities are there for your career and promotion?

Notes

1
See, for example, Hersey, Blanchard and Johnson (2001).
2
See, for example, Blanchard, Zigarmi and Zigarmi (1985), Hersey (1985) and Hersey, Blanchard and Johnson (2001).
3
See Laurent (1986).
4
One of the Worldwork international competency set.

Chapter 7
Communication

Constructing meaning | 7.1

Verbal communication consists of encoding and sending messages through language, and receiving and decoding these messages. Messages do not usually *contain* a single objective meaning. Rather, messages *are given* meaning first by the sender (or encoder) and then in turn by the receiver (or decoder).

In this way, we can say that two people who communicate with each other *construct* meaning – on two different building sites! The meaning given to the message by each person on these two different sites is rarely exactly the same and this is how miscommunication occurs. When you are communicating across cultures, the chances of miscommunication occurring are even greater.

People sometimes replace and often support verbal communication with non-verbal messages using body language. This can sometimes help communication across cultures but it can also make it more difficult.

Tuning into body language | 7.2

When you are working internationally, communication through language often becomes more difficult and less effective for those who are not using their first language. So understanding body language becomes more important than at home. Mindful international managers must learn to read the signals communicated in other ways than through language.

Your interpretation of these signals will enrich and support your understanding of the verbal message to create clearer meaning in a complex communication situation. But remember that the non-verbal signals you notice may not have the same meaning as they do in your own culture.

Key competence
Perceptiveness through being attuned[1]
Being attuned to non-verbal signals is an ability of effective international managers. They are focused on picking up meaning from signals such as intonation, eye contact and body language. They can interpret such signals correctly in different cultures.

Eye contact
Be careful to observe the nature of eye contact which is common in a culture new to you. Westerners should not assume that you must make and maintain eye contact. In some cultures, people hold eye contact. In others, people make eye contact but do not hold it. Westerners should *not* interpret a lack of steady eye contact as a sign of untrustworthiness. In some cultures, the conventions for eye contact are different for men and for women.

Physical distance between people

Observe the distances people maintain when standing or sitting next to each other. For example, in Latin cultures people may like to stay closer to each other and to have some physical contact. In some other cultures, a greater distance can be maintained and no physical contact made at all.

Facial expression

In some cultures, it is the norm for people to show clearly what they feel – to show that they are happy or upset, by smiling, frowning, and so on. In some cultures, people maintain neutral facial expressions and the preference is for people to hide what they feel. In other cultures, people may smile a lot in order to hide their real feelings.

Greeting rituals

The mindful international manager knows that, in some cultures, rituals attached to meeting somebody for the first time and to greeting business acquaintances are important. This is especially true in settings relatively uninfluenced by international business. You should give greeting rituals time and attention here.

Observe who shakes hands with whom, and who kisses whom, and how many times. In France, the morning greetings at work are important. Managers may go round the office, shaking hands with everyone in the team and perhaps kissing some of them. In some Muslim countries, men and women do not usually shake hands. The importance attached to business cards and the way we exchange them also differ across cultures.

I'm very informal. But in the Hong Kong context one has to be a bit careful about being informal too soon. Certainly middle-aged Chinese people expect a certain degree of formality to begin with in terms of both address, how you use names, etc., and dress, what you wear and how you hold yourself and so on.

John Duncan (U.K.), educational consultant, Hong Kong

Of course, as an outsider, you will not necessarily be expected to behave like a member of the culture which you are visiting. But local people may appreciate your ability to adapt to an appropriate extent to local behaviour, especially if you are a frequent or long-term visitor to the place in question.

A more difficult situation is meeting an international group – for example, members of a project team from all over the world – away from your home location – where there is no clear and established norm for greetings.

Taking turns at speaking | 7.3

Communicating across cultures is difficult not only because body language is different in different cultures. Individuals contribute to conversations and discussions in meetings in different ways. Some people allow you to finish before they start to speak. Others speak at the same time. Others allow a moment of silence before speaking.

We tend to make judgements about deviations from our own way of taking turns. To some people, interrupters seem pushy, but to others they seem lively. To some people, those who wait to speak seem polite, but to others they seem reserved and even boring.

These different ways of taking over from another speaker – taking turns – can be driven by personality, but also by cultural background. Our judgements about turn-taking conventions can be the product of our personality but also of our culture.

In which cultures do you think people tend to speak like this?
The answers[2] are in the notes at then end of the chapter.

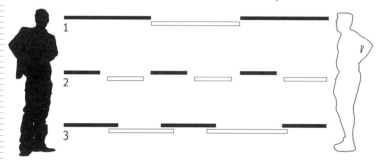

Adapted from Trompenaars (1993)

One influence on turn-taking styles could be how people use time. In cultures with a tendency to structure time and do one thing at a time, turn-taking may be structured more formally. In these cultures, turns tend to occur when someone finishes talking and another starts – without overlapping or pausing (as in example 1 above). In cultures with a more fluid approach to time, the turns tend to overlap and people tend to speak at the same time (see example 3 above).

So we need to try and make sense of people's body language in a new cultural context. We also need to pay attention to how people hand over and take over communication when they are talking. However, the language itself is perhaps the aspect of communication which is most likely to cause difficulties.

Using language to create understanding | 7.4

When you communicate across cultures, you must not assume that your message will be easily understood.

Getting messages across in a meeting taking place in a language everybody speaks as their mother tongue is difficult enough. Even here, it is rare for everybody to understand the same thing.

In an international meeting taking place in a lingua franca (often English), which only some or none speak as their first language, 'full' understanding is rarer. People who nod their heads may seem to understand but they may be doing so more for reasons of politeness than of comprehension.

Research shows that non-native speakers of English working with native speakers often feel confused and frustrated by the sophisticated language their native speaker colleagues may use. They may also be annoyed by the inability or unwillingness of native speakers to simplify the language they use to help their non-native colleagues understand more easily.

> *The English aren't always sympathetic to Germans when they speak English.*
> *To begin with, the English speak slowly, but then fall back into speaking the*
> *same speed and slang as if the listener is a native.*
> HR manager (Germany), power generation, Germany

Non-native speakers sometimes see this inability of native speakers to adapt their language as a deliberate and unfair tactic to push through some course of action.

International managers need to be mindful of the very complex communication situation they are in and to adjust their language accordingly.[3]

If their English is more advanced, they need to create clarity for the other party, in particular by simplifying their language. If their English is less advanced, they can also use special techniques to create clarity.

Clarity skills for native or advanced speakers
- speak more clearly and slowly than usual
- pause and emphasise key words
- increase redundancy, i.e. repeat and paraphrase
- avoid unnecessarily technical words, slang, idioms
- restrict the range of your vocabulary
- use short sentences
- use transparent sentence structure,
  e.g. *He asked if he could leave*, not *He asked to leave*
- avoid contractions, e.g. *I'll, shouldn't've*
- use labelling language, e.g. *I'd like to make a suggestion.*
  There are three possible actions: firstly, … ; secondly, … ; thirdly, …
- use more yes / no questions
- provide answers for the interlocutor to choose from,
  e.g. *We can set up the equipment in two ways: like this …*
  and like that … Which do you prefer?

Clarity skills for less advanced or non-native speakers

> speak clearly and slowly
> pause and emphasise key words
> increase redundancy, i.e. repeat and paraphrase
> do not translate word for word from your first language
> use 'prefabs' (prefabricated expressions), i.e. phrases and sentences
  learnt by heart to gain thinking time
> ask for repetitions and explanations
> ask your interlocutor to speak more clearly, slowly and simply
> ask your interlocutor to remember that you are using a foreign language

Non-native speakers of English working together in English are using a common language as a tool of communication and often find it easier to understand each other than native speakers.

Key competence
Transparency through clarity of communication
Creating clarity in their communication is a central ability of effective international managers. They understand that in international situations the potential for misunderstanding is high and thus the need for clarity is especially great. Native speakers work to make their language transparent and easily understood by those less fluent in the language in question. They are able to do this without appearing to talk down to people. Non-native speakers pronounce clearly and slowly.

Listening actively to create understanding | 7.5

Not only does intercultural communication require *clarity* skills to create understanding. It crucially also requires *active listening* skills. Showing you are listening by maintaining the right amount of eye contact and nodding, for example, are basic listening skills.

Strangely, true active listening also means speaking in the right way to create understanding and negotiate meaning. You should check not just whether your interlocutor has understood but whether *you* have. And when you realise that a misunderstanding has occurred, you need to repair it. Summarising what you have understood is also an active listening skill. If you get it wrong, the other side has the opportunity to correct misunderstandings.

Communicating like this takes time. International communication usually takes longer. However, mindful managers realise that attention paid to the process will improve the outcome. The end result is greater clarity and better understanding and this will save time later.

Key competence
Active listening[1]

Effective international managers not only listen carefully but also show they are doing so, for example by maintaining eye contact, nodding or taking notes. They clarify by summarising and paraphrasing not only what they have said but what they understand others have said. When they see a misunderstanding has occurred, they pro-actively negotiate meaning with their interlocutor to create understanding.

There seems to have been a misunderstanding.

Communicating, socialising and building relationships | 7.6

Whether we like it or not, socialising is an important part of building relationships. We may socialise both during and after work. During work, it may be over lunch or a coffee or a birthday cake. After work, it could be a drink, a meal in a restaurant or a larger celebration.

Attitudes towards interpersonal distance and therefore also socialising are very culturally influenced (see Chapter 2). How much socialising takes place with colleagues and the setting chosen for it may thus differ greatly, not only from culture to culture but also from person to person.

As an international manager you need to be sensitive and flexible in this area.

Peaches and coconuts

Peaches have soft outsides which are easy to bite into. Coconuts have hard outsides which can be difficult to crack. In what Susanne Zaninelli[4] calls a coconut culture, colleagues tend to keep their work life and their private, non-work life separate from each other. Social conversation at work may be relatively rare.

People in coconut cultures feel that they should not invade your personal space, either physically or mentally. They may seem unfriendly and unapproachable to peaches but their behaviour aims to express respect for your privacy. You may have to take the initiative in showing that you want to get to know them, even if you are the visitor.

When a peach meets a coconut

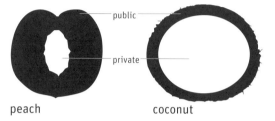

peach   coconut

Adapted from Lewin (1936), Trompenaars (1993) and Zaninelli(1994)

On the other hand, in a peach culture, you may be expected to socialise a lot at or after work and even at the weekends. Peach-like cultures may see relationships as short-term and their friendliness must not be mistaken by coconuts for a sign of lifelong friendship.

I try to build up a sort of 'Let's do something after work' whenever possible. In the office I'm trying to get to know what they're doing, to get involved in their talks, and now I'm starting to talk Turkish a little bit, only a few words and always try to say a few words in Turkish.
Luis Ortega (Spain), Henkel, Turkey

You are more likely to be invited to somebody's home in a peach-like culture. They are usually more willing to share their personal living space with you more quickly. The more peach-like the culture, the more of their lives they will share with you – for example, you may be allowed to move around their homes, sit and talk to them in the kitchen, and help yourself to a drink from the refrigerator.

Peaches are also more likely to share personal information about themselves and expect you to do the same – their likes and dislikes, the trouble they are having with their children, even their marriages.

The ability to make small talk or social conversation is a must in peach-like cultures as it helps to build relationships and is what happens during socialising activities. You must not only talk about work.

Analyse how you make social conversation
Assess on a scale from 1 (very little) to 7 (very much)
the extent to which you ...

listen for personal information that your interlocutor drops into the conversation and refer to it in your contributions to the small talk as a way of connecting with the person.

1 2 3 4 5 6 7

offer personal information in passing which your interlocutor can build on in the same way.

1 2 3 4 5 6 7

seek common ground – experiences, interests, views you share – with your interlocutor.

1 2 3 4 5 6 7

integrate and connect the experiences and views of your interlocutor with your own rather than seeking contrasts.

1 2 3 4 5 6 7

remember that opinions are merely opinions, and not facts which can be right or wrong.

1 2 3 4 5 6 7

ask open questions rather than closed questions.

1 2 3 4 5 6 7

look and sound interested even if your interlocutor is a complete bore!

1 2 3 4 5 6 7

Speaking transparently and listening effectively | 7.7

Good communication skills underpin all your interactions when working internationally.

Speaking transparently

Because there is such a high risk of communication breakdown, you need to work very hard to be transparent. This means not just clearly communicating your *message* but also the *intention* behind it.

Instead of communicating the message like this:
I'd like that report by the end of the day.
describe your intention as well and say:
> *I'd like that report by the end of the day. It's very important for me to have time to read it before the meeting tomorrow.*

Instead of communicating the message like this:
I disagree with you.
describe your intention as well and say:
> *I disagree with you. It's nothing personal. I just think there is another way to do it.*

Instead of communicating the message like this:
We need to all work harder.
describe your intention as well and say:
> *I've been thinking about this and I've come to the conclusion that we all need to work harder. It's the only way we will survive.*

It also means *structuring* and *labelling* your communication as clearly as possible.

If you're giving a presentation say:
> *I've divided it into three parts.*
and then clearly signpost the three parts.

If you're running a meeting say:
> *There are three items on the agenda.*
and then clearly signpost where you are in the meeting.

If you're on the telephone say:
> *I've got two points. The first is …*
and clearly signpost the points.

The secret is to tell them what you're going to say, say it and then to tell them what you've said.

For native speakers of English, it means avoiding idioms, and jokes which non-native speakers may not follow, and remembering how hard it is for your colleagues to communicate in a foreign language.

> *There are still quite big differences to the UK so my getting to know*
> *strategies, humour, irony, laughing a little at myself, were viewed with*
> *some surprise by my Chinese colleagues at the beginning.*
> John Duncan (U.K.), educational consultant, Hong Kong

Listening effectively
The other side of the coin is how well you listen. Good listening is not only a way to communicate better but also helps to build relationships. One way we can do this is by using the language of active listening.

The language of active listening
Here are some ways of using language to listen actively:

Showing you are listening
> *Right*
> *OK*
> *I see*

Testing your own understanding
> *If I am not mistaken, you are saying …*
> *What I have understood is …*
> *Correct me if I'm wrong but what you're saying is …*

Testing the understanding of your interlocutor
> *Did I get that across OK?*
> *Shall I repeat that?*

Summarising
> *Let me go over that again*
> *Just to recap:*

Repairing misunderstanding
> *There seems to have been a misunderstanding.*
> *I think we may be getting something wrong.*
> *Let me correct a false impression.*

Notes
1
One of the Worldwork international competency set.
2
Answer: 1. e.g. Germany, UK, 2. e.g. Finland, Japan, 3. e.g. Italy, Spain.
3
See Spencer-Oatey and Franklin (forthcoming).
4
See Zaninelli (1994).

Feedback

This chapter focuses on

how feedback which you give
in the right way can motivate and
develop people

how culture and personality affect
attitudes towards feedback and the
way people give and receive it

how the international manager
can achieve higher performance
through mindful feedback

Formal and informal feedback |

Feedback is a process of observing and then commenting on people's behaviours and skills in order to maintain or improve their performance. Feedback in organisations can be managed in two ways.

Formally

Many organisations have a formal process of performance review or apprais-al. This often take place on a regular basis (for example, annually). It involves looking at past performance and then setting targets for future performance. It often relates to business objectives but, when well done, can also pay attention to personal preferences and attitudes. Some companies widen the scope of appraisal by introducing a 360° feedback process, in which manag-ers, colleagues and reports all give feedback (often anonymously in writing).

Many managers and their reports complain that such formal feedback is just 'ticking the boxes'. In other words, it is a process they have to follow but do not believe in.

Informally

In this case, people give feedback when they note good or poor performance. For example, you hear a colleague give a good presentation and you comment on this afterwards. Or, you notice a member of your staff has been making mistakes in his work and you ask him what is wrong.

This type of feedback can be much more important for the receiver of the feedback than formal feedback. It is more immediate because it happens soon after the performance that the manager is commenting on. And it shows that managers notice the performance, behaviours, skills and moods of their team members. Feedback given immediately after the action assessed may more often lead to changes in behaviour.

I like – with people I work with – to be able to reflect on ourselves once in a while, not very often but sometimes. And this is an important quality of a team. If you can look at yourself, see what you've done, clarify things and then go back to work. This helps me a lot and makes me feel good in a team. So I need open feedback processes. That's part of my team style.

Torsten Weber (Germany), HLP, Germany

Although national and organisational cultures greatly influence the giving and receiving of feedback, managers should recognise that everybody can profit from feedback of some kind or another. Everyone needs feedback to do better.

Culture and feedback |

Performance management and the role which feedback has to play in this are a cultural minefield. There are several key cultural dimensions which can affect the nature of the feedback people give and how people receive it.

Task orientation and relationship orientation

Creating a feedback culture may be easier in environments in which organisations are seen as instruments for managing tasks rather than as systems of social relationships. Some organisational and national or ethnic cultures encourage very task-oriented behaviour. This means that people are expected to be very focused and specific about what they are doing. They need to know the what, the where, the why and the how. Managers expect employees to perform tasks to a high standard as long as they clearly understand what they have to do.

In these types of culture, people often only give feedback when something goes wrong. Having everything going right is the norm so there is no need to comment positively on it.

On the other hand, people in organisational cultures which are less task-oriented but more focused on relationships tend to do things for other reasons as well: because they want to be cooperative, or to show integrity, or because they are friends with their colleagues or feel loyal to their organisation. Of course, they need to understand the specifics of the task too. They will do it well if they want to and these more personal, relationship-related factors are key.

In these types of culture, there is often a need for supportive or encouraging feedback and you have to be careful about giving critical feedback as it may easily offend people.

Communication orientation

In cultures which prefer direct communication (see Chapter 2), people tend to be more prepared to give and receive feedback. They may be happy to receive positive feedback in a group or in front of their colleagues. They may be more willing to receive critical feedback on a one-to-one basis.

In cultures where people communicate less directly, it can be more difficult to give or receive direct feedback. It may be necessary to speak to people on a one-to-one basis to find out what they are thinking. Even this will not be a transparent process without trust and understanding between you.

If you travel to North America, they may give much more direct feedback than anywhere else in the world. If you are not used to it, then you could sense it as rather hostile or aggressive. In Asia you have the complete opposite.

Ulrich Hansen (Germany), Henkel, Germany

Power orientation

The giving and receiving of feedback – especially 360 degree feedback – may depend on a relationship between the giver and receiver which allows

dialogue to take place on more or less equal terms. The power difference between the two parties may need to be relatively small.

Group-orientation – individualism

Giving feedback as practised in, say, British and US organisations, is based on the belief that performance is the result of individual effort and that individuals can be held responsible for good or bad performance. This may clash with group-oriented notions of responsibility in other cultures.

Face and feedback | 8.3

A very significant influencing factor in more group-oriented cultures is the concept of face. The need to protect face is important for all members of the group. A person can lose face as a result of losing his or her temper, confronting an individual, acting in an arrogant manner or failing to show appropriate respect.

What does the concept of face mean in practice?

> Relationships are long-term and need to be cultivated. This means that you cannot afford to have serious conflicts with someone in your in-group.

> The reputation of your family and colleagues can be affected positively or negatively by your own reputation. Criticism is therefore not just a matter of an individual accepting and learning from it. The criticism can be seen to affect other people.

> There is a commonly held fear of standing out from the group, of not fitting in or of being criticised, ridiculed or reprimanded in public. This means that you need to be careful about focusing on individuals either for praise or criticism.

You can never ever surprise or embarrass a Baltic manager in a meeting in front of his colleagues because then he's lost. And that's part of the culture.

Erik Hallberg (Sweden), TeliaSonera, Sweden

Personality and feedback | 8.4

Feedback is also a very personal issue. Most people are sensitive about receiving critical feedback. Some people are suspicious about receiving positive feedback.

Sincerity

People need to feel the feedback they receive is sincere. The more introverted their preferred behaviour is, the more sensitive they may be about feedback. Extroverts often accept feedback at face value – it could be that the feedback is superficial but that does not matter. More introverted people find superficial feedback insincere and may well only welcome feedback which is properly considered. The best way of making sure this happens is to get the receiver of the feedback to reflect upon his or her own performance.

Self-reflection

The starting point for much personal development is self-reflection – holding the mirror up to ourselves. We need to see ourselves clearly and also through the eyes of others. The person giving the feedback has a vital role in helping us to see the gap between where we are and where we want to be and also taking action to get there.

The manager who is skilled in the feedback process will rarely just say "That was good. I like the way you presented the issue" or "That could have been better. I thought you should have been better prepared." He/she will ask the team member "How did you think that went?" or "What do you think went well?"

In this way, the feedback comes from self-reflection and is much more powerful and much more likely to lead to change.

Types of feedback | 8.5

Q: Can we start with a basic question? What is feedback exactly?

A: For me, you give feedback when you want someone to develop, to be better. But it's only on behaviour, not personality. And if you want to give feedback, you have to check if the person really can change it or not, if it really is a behaviour.

Dani Stromberg (Sweden), management consultant, Sweden

There are two types of feedback used for increasing the performance of teams and individuals.

Affirmative feedback

In this case, the manager observes a team member contributing to the success of the team. This may be because of the quality of work on a certain task or it could be through hard work and dedication over time. It is important to follow these steps:

Three-step affirmative feedback

1 Say what you have observed.
> *I've noticed how hard you have been working these last few weeks.*

2 Say what effect this behaviour has.
> *This has meant that we have reached some demanding deadlines.*

3 Show appreciation and encouragement.
> *Thank you for all your efforts. Your work is really making a difference.*

Clearly, you can give affirmative feedback to the team as well as to individuals.

Developmental feedback

In this case, the manager observes an individual or the team having difficulty with a task or not performing to their potential. It is important to follow these steps:

Three-step developmental feedback

1 Say what you have observed.
> *I noticed that the quality has dropped in this area.*

2 Say what effect this behaviour has.
> *This means we are having to repeat a lot of tasks.*

3 Say what change you want to see.
> *We need to focus on each step more carefully.*

Over a longer period of time of several months what do you think the balance should be between these types of feedback?

1. a ratio of 50 affirmative : 50 development

2. a ratio of 20 affirmative : 80 development

3. a ratio of 60 affirmative : 40 development

Of course it depends on the situation – is your team doing a good job or not? However, if you want them to accept the development feedback, it is very important to recognise good performance when you see it – the 60:40 ratio is a good guideline.

Best practice
Balancing transparency and harmony | 8.6

While recognising the importance of feedback in achieving performance, mindful international managers are also aware of the implications of cultural values and norms for the giving and receiving of feedback. It is probably the most sensitive task in interpersonal terms that international managers working with numerous cultures have to deal with.

The fundamental challenge is to take account of both the need for honesty and transparency, and the need for harmonious relationships – needs which vary across cultures. In every culture, you need to get a message across, but you also need to make sure that relationships remain sound. The damage that can be done to relationships by transparency varies from culture to culture.

In some cultures more than in others, it is difficult to separate the *transactional* from the *relational*. Where relationships are damaged by too much transparency (from the viewpoint of the receiver of the feedback), the feedback may lead to negative feelings and to demotivation. It may thus not only fail to improve performance but even actually have the reverse effect.

Giving individual feedback – both affirmative feedback and developmental feedback – may contribute to improved individual performance in individualistic, task-oriented cultures with small hierarchical differences. In very strongly task-oriented cultures, people may see affirmative feedback as superfluous and even insincere. For example, the hamburger approach of surrounding the meat of the developmental feedback with the soft roll of the affirmative feedback will not necessarily be effective. In such cultures, you can often give developmental feedback in a direct and open fashion.

In more group-oriented cultures which value face and harmony, feedback needs to be given less transparently, so that the face of the individual and the harmony of the group are preserved. Notice that as the feedback below progresses from down the page, it becomes less transparent and so more likely not to be a threat to face and harmony.

Reducing transparency in the interest of harmony
Talk about a person's actions rather than about the person's shortcomings
Don't say: *You forgot to deal with south-east Asia in the report.*
➤ Say: *You omitted south-east Asia in the report.*

Use a negative plus a positive verb rather than just a negative verb
Don't say: *You omitted south-east Asia in the report.*
➤ Say: *You didn't deal with south-east Asia in the report.*

Remove the feedback receiver by emphasising the feedback giver
Don't say: *You didn't deal with south-east Asia in the report.*
➤ Say: *I couldn't find the section on south east Asia.*

Remove the feedback receiver and the feedback giver by emphasising the message
Don't say: *You didn't deal with south-east Asia in the report* or
I couldn't find the section on south east Asia.
➤ Say: *The section on south-east Asia is missing.*

Use down-toners, such as *seem, appear, apparently, unfortunately, I'm afraid*
Don't say: *The section on south-east Asia is missing.*
➤ Say: *I'm afraid the section on south-east Asia seems to be missing.*

Writing of Thailand, Paul Verluyten[1] recommends the use of *blurring techniques*:

➤ Blur the receiver. Give negative feedback to the whole group and not to the individual.
➤ Blur the sender. Use a third party – a friend or a colleague – to pass on the criticism.
➤ Blur the message. Talk about a hypothetical case to direct the feedback receiver's attention to the cause of the negative criticism.

These techniques can also be used to make feedback more indirect and to preserve harmony.

Notes
1
Verluyten (1999).

Chapter 9

Conflict

This chapter focuses on

understanding personal and cultural attitudes towards conflict

approaches to preventing conflict

approaches to resolving conflict

identifying best practices for dealing with conflict across cultures

Personal attitudes
towards conflict | 9.1

One person's conflict is another person's debate. In other words, what people see as a conflict can vary enormously. In this chapter, we mean by conflict a breakdown in a working relationship caused by one or more people feeling strongly about an event or an ongoing situation. An event could be a meeting in which someone speaks rudely or it could be a failure to do a piece of work that had been agreed on. An ongoing situation could be a lack of support in a demanding role. These events or situations upset us and engage our emotions. We can feel anger, hatred, resentment or jealousy.

If we do not address the cause of the conflict, the feelings could go away – our emotions could gradually diminish. Or they could remain, slowly eating away at our motivation, enjoyment and performance.

Avoiding conflict
Some people are very skilled at disguising their feelings so it is difficult to see that there is a breakdown in the relationship. Many people do not want to face a conflict – the thought of bringing the conflict into the open is even worse than continuing to suffer from it. Maybe their experience is that trying to resolve the conflict can be more damaging than pretending everything is okay. This conclusion may be based on other conflicts they have experienced or on their lack of skill in dealing with conflict.

Facing conflict
Other people believe it is always better to face a conflict and try to resolve it. While the conflict is there, they cannot work or concentrate up to their usual standard. It robs them of their motivation and focus. Even if they may know that it will be difficult or even impossible to resolve the conflict, they try to achieve this because they feel it is better than doing nothing. Unfortunately if they try without the necessary skill, it may be difficult for them to resolve the conflict. In fact, they could make it worse.

What is your attitude towards conflict?

A colleague arrives late. You are going to miss a travel connection. You feel she has been selfish – she should have called you to keep you informed.
Do you criticise her for being late?

One of your colleagues in the team is always dominating meetings. You have some really good ideas but you find it difficult to get them heard. You wish the project leader would shut him up. However, you don't believe this will happen.
Do you raise the issue with the dominating colleague?

Your boss shows favouritism towards a colleague. He gives her a lot of attention and also the most interesting jobs to do. You feel undervalued and more and more resentful.
Do you raise this issue with your boss or someone else or not at all?

Different orientations to conflict are pictured in the grid below. At the heart of this picture of orientations to conflict is the question: Are you more interested in satisfying your own interests (self-centred) or those of the other party (other-centred)?

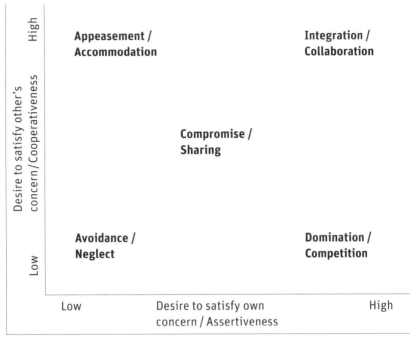

Thomas's 'grid' framework of conflict management orientations
Adapted from Thomas (1976) and Spencer-Oatey and Franklin (forthcoming)

If you have no desire to give in to the other party to the conflict but if you are also not interested in settling the conflict in your own interest, you will be located in the bottom left-hand corner (avoidance).

If you are prepared to give up and satisfy the other party at the expense of yourself, you can be found in the top left-hand corner (appeasement / accommodation).

Domination / competition (bottom right-hand corner) is an orientation in which parties to conflict seeks to get their own way at all costs. Integration (top right-hand corner) seeks to satisfy both parties by applying a problem-solving approach.

 How do you prefer to manage conflict?
Locate your preferred orientation on the grid.

Most people have a hierarchy of orientations and choose the preferred approach depending on the particular conflict. This hierarchy may be influenced by culturally based preferences.

Culturally influenced attitudes towards conflict | 9.2

Belonging to a certain culture – national, business or other grouping – helps us to define our identity and gives us the security of belonging to a group. Unfortunately, people tend to define identity in contrast to another group. Finance as opposed to marketing, German rather than American, Microsoft not Apple. This provides the context for a lot of conflict. When cultures are closed to outsiders, they may become defensive and see difference as a threat.

As we have seen in Chapter 8, the mindful international manager needs to be careful not to blame cultural preferences for conflict. Often, personality or the situation are much more to blame for a breakdown in a relationship. However, culture does have a large impact on how we view and resolve conflicts.

Michelle LeBaron and Bruce Grundison[1] report the following:

In an interview conducted in Canada, an elderly Chinese man indicated that he had experienced no conflict at all for the previous forty years.

Group-oriented cultures tend to view and deal with conflict differently from individualistic cultures. Stella Ting-Toomey[2] describes how, in individualistic cultures, people usually identify the source of conflict as being personal. They tend to believe that resolution can be achieved through focusing on outcomes which will satisfy the individuals concerned as far as possible.

People from more group-oriented cultures see restraint of personal emotions as key to protecting face and maintaining long-term relationships. This has priority over achieving particular goals in the resolution of conflict.

Assumptions about conflict

In individualistic cultures, …	In group-oriented cultures, …
conflict is outcome oriented, i.e. people in conflict want to achieve goals	conflict is process-oriented, i.e. people in conflict want to preserve face before dealing with goals
satisfying communication in the conflict means bringing the conflict out into the open and sharing feelings honestly and assertively	satisfying communication in the conflict involves both face-saving and face-giving and paying attention to both verbal and non-verbal messages
conflict outcomes are productive when tangible solutions are reached	conflict process or outcomes are productive when face on both sides is saved and substantive agreement is reached

Behaviour in conflict

In conflicts in individualistic cultures people tend to ...	In conflicts in group-oriented cultures people tend to ...
express strong personal opinions	express the opinions of the group
display their emotions	restrain emotions
take personal responsibility for the source of the conflict	protect members of the group from being held personally responsible

Advice for individualists in conflict with people from a more group-oriented culture
> Be patient
> Listen actively but also reflectively
> Be prepared to listen to stories which do not seem relevant
> Use questions which allow your colleagues to help or advise you ("What do you think we should do?")
> Focus on the group, not individuals

There was a very nasty man called Habib and he found a very small palm tree growing in the desert. He didn't like to see it growing there so he put a large stone on top of it. The palm tree tried hard to survive and the stone pushed its roots deeper and deeper until it found water. As a result, it grew and grew to be a very large palm tree. Habib returned some years later. He didn't recognise the tree until he looked upwards and saw the stone perched on its top.

(Story told by Khaltoum Feiler during intercultural conflict training)

Advice for collectivists in conflict with people from a more individualistic culture
> Be assertive about personal interests and goals
> Listen actively, especially to the content of the message
> Clearly indicate responses (positive and negative) and also reasoning
> Use questions to clarify in order to be more specific
> Focus on individuals, less on the group.

Preventing conflict through effective communication | 9.3

A lot of communication is email and we all communicate in a language which is not our mother tongue. That can cause problems because you can read between the lines something that was never meant. Maybe someone writes something quickly, thinking it is good English and I read it as a command or a criticism just because of not using the right words. A lot of misunderstanding is possible.

Wibke Kuhnert (Germany), Henkel, U.S.A.

When working internationally it is necessary to be mindful of the channel of communication, the style of communication, and the language of communication.

The channel of communication

The most common channel of communication in international business is email. Although it is very efficient, it can also be very damaging. It may be acceptable to write short, sharp emails to local colleagues whom you know well. However, mindful international managers need to realise that short, sharp emails can reach your partners abroad at a bad moment or can easily be misunderstood.

> Do not use email to communicate complex or sensitive messages or give negative feedback. Send an email to book a telephone call at an appropriate time.
> Never respond to an email too quickly. If you find yourself getting angry or upset on reading an email, take a break. Reply to the email the next day.
> Use the phone more often in order to build and cultivate relationships and also to make sure your messages are getting across.
> Do not copy your emails to cover yourself. It may display a lack of trust in your partner.

The style of communication

In international work settings, the style of communication becomes very critical to building relationships and avoiding conflict. When managers work at home, people see them and get to know them – they may be forgiven if they are sometimes very direct or rather bossy. Getting the style wrong when working internationally can be disastrous.

Personal / Impersonal

If you are very personal in your style of communication, you may need to vary your style and make sure you can communicate more impersonally – or the other way round. An over-personal approach may not be appreciated by more coconut-like cultures (see Chapter 7). On the other hand, in more relationship-oriented cultures, it may be necessary to focus on the personal.

The Turkish way of doing business means you have to be close, to know about their personal situation. Then people will listen to you and are open to accepting proposals.

Luis Ortega (Spain), Henkel, Turkey

Direct / Indirect

If you tend to be direct in your style of communication, you may need to vary your style and make sure you can communicate more indirectly. An over-direct approach may not be appreciated by more indirect cultures (see Chapter 2) and can lead to loss of face, disharmony and damage to the relationship. On the other hand, in a more direct culture, you need to say what you are thinking.

Q: Well, what does 'yes' mean in a Pakistani context?

A: Yes doesn't necessarily mean yes. I don't really know what it means but there are no guarantees. People think the important thing is to have the client and take the problems later on. I was in Pakistan two weeks ago and everywhere in any kind of business they deal like this. They say "Yes we can do it". They never say no.

Sherri Warsi (Pakistan), Integrico, Sweden

The language of communication

We saw in Chapter 7 some of the problems connected with using English as a lingua franca. Native and non-native speakers need to realise how powerful language can be. Just one word can set off a conflict.

Compare *'We expected better results'* with *'We forecast better results'*. 'Expect' is more personal and may suggest that somebody is responsible for 'poor' results.

When using English as an international language, managers cannot afford to be too sensitive about language. They need to use English as a tool but not as a weapon.

Preventing conflict through understanding the context | 9.4

The mindful international manager needs to understand the often conflicting interests which may exist in any business situation in order to prevent conflict arising.

You may find that in hierarchical cultures, you need to involve bosses directly but discreetly. If these cultures also have a strong group-orientation, they will not want their employees singled out. In international projects it is important to open these channels from the start. The project manager needs to speak to the line managers of all project members before the project starts.

Conflict can often arise between local and international priorities. A local manager can be squeezed in both directions – by his local boss to achieve local targets and by his project leader to achieve international results. If you establish contact with local bosses, this can help avoid conflict arising later.

Resolving conflicts:
some options | 9.5

There are various ways of handling conflicts:

Approaches to managing conflict

Approach	Advantages[3]	Disadvantages[3]	Appropriate in what kinds of culture?
Ignore	cooling off possible; time heals; outward harmony preserved	things may get worse	face-saving, harmony seeking, group oriented, relationship-oriented
Confront directly	clarity and understanding created; those involved find the solution and thus are more committed to it	commitment to process may be incomplete; process can be emotional and subjective	direct communication, task-oriented, individualist, non-hierarchical
Involve a third party	harmony preserved; conflict addressed, even solved	possibly incomplete understanding of the conflict	face-saving, harmony seeking, group-oriented, relationship-oriented
Involve the team	more and better solutions; a decision made by a team is strong and not authoritarian	loss of face is possible; really critical issues avoided in the group	direct communication, task-oriented, individualist, non-hierarchical
Escalate / appeal to authority	may be effective and efficient in urgent cases	win-lose outcome; loser may feel devalued and lose face	hierarchical

Adapted from Bennett (1995) and Spencer-Oatey and Franklin (forthcoming)

Ignore
This approach may be the best option if you are working in a culture where this is the usual practice in order to maintain harmony. Consider the advantages and disadvantages of this option. If you feel the conflict is affecting performance, you may need to move on to one of the other options.

Confront directly
This technique is often the first instinct of US or German managers. Bring the conflict out into the open and deal directly with the person. Don't involve intermediaries. You may expect people to be frank but in many cultures, people will be unwilling to be so.

Involve a third party

The third party – a colleague or a superior – will talk to the parties individually but not together. This means that the two people who are in conflict do not have to meet together initially. This saves face and maintains harmony.

So people often try to calm the waters, to do things through a third party or behind the scenes, or just sitting down and talking and trying to solve problems in a spirit of understanding.

Brian Cracknell (UK), Language Works, Malaysia

Involve the team

This approach is used by some Western managers. The group discusses the conflict and together the members offer support to both parties and suggest solutions. People need to handle this option very sensitively. It would not work if individuals feel exposed in the group. There is some risk of loss of face.

Escalate the issue and appeal to authority

This means taking the issue higher up in the organisation in order to involve someone with more power and authority. This person then settles the conflict by imposing a solution. People in more hierarchical cultures, where decision-making is always pushed upwards, may favour this approach.

As soon as there was a conflict, instead of dealing directly with the person, they take it to the boss. And I think they should come and talk to me first and I will try to explain why. The reason they do it is that they want to be on the safe side. They send lots of mails up just to show later on that this wasn't our fault.

Sherri Warsi (Pakistan), Integrico Sweden

Which is the best option?

It is important not to think that there is a single right way to solve a conflict. There are some underlying skills (see below) but there is no universal approach. You need to reflect on your preferences and those of the people you are working with, observe how others deal with conflict, and extend your range of approaches.

Yourself, the others and trust | 9.6

Reflect on yourself
Effective and mindful conflict management starts with yourself. If you know how others see you, this helps you to understand them and take their perspective.

Key competence
Perceptiveness through reflected awareness[4]
Being aware of how members of other cultures see them is a quality of effective international managers. They understand how their culture influences their attitudes and behaviour and that this may be strange and difficult for the people they work with internationally. They are sensitive to how their behaviour is interpreted by their business partners.

Q: Were the conflicts you experienced related to culture, personality or working styles?
A: It's a good question because you can't always say that the problem is due to the fact that this is an American or a German. It depends so much more on the personality. And so self-awareness, of your own personality, is really important. You need to know how you are perceived, what aspects of your culture you exhibit, and what kind of impact that it might have on other people, and to be open to these things.
Wibke Kuhnert (Germany), Henkel, U.S.A.

Display an ability to take the perspective of the other party to the conflict
It may be possible for each side to demonstrate that it understands the position of the other party to the conflict. This does not mean the two sides agree but they must show that they can see why the other side has arrived at this position. Understanding of this kind is the basis of much conflict resolution.

Preserve face – theirs and yours.
It is very important to separate the person from the issue – if this is possible, because sometimes the person *is* the issue. If either party feels that the conflict is an attack on his or her personally, it will be very difficult to resolve. In some cultures, indirect and implicit communication is necessary to maintain face and harmony, especially in public. In more direct cultures, it is possible to be more explicit, but even so, it is important to be aware of individual sensitivities.

Build trust
It is possible to resolve a conflict if both parties believe that the other side will keep to the agreed resolution of the conflict and that this will make a difference in the future. The strength of this belief depends on the existence of trust among the parties to the conflict. Trust reduces the uncertainty which naturally occurs in any kind of cooperation or interaction. This uncertainty is all the greater if people come from different cultures or work in virtual teams – or are in conflict!

Ideas about trust vary across cultures: competence, benevolence, integrity, predictability and openness with information are some of the things that can lead to the creation of trust (see Chapter 10). Work at finding out what kind of trust is important for your international partners. If you have built the right kind of trust, it will be easier to resolve conflicts when they occur.

Notes

1

See LeBaron and Bruce (1993).

2

See Ting-Toomey (1999).

3

See Bennett (1995).

4

One of the Worldwork international competency set.

Chapter 10
Cooperation

The basis for cooperation |

Cooperating with colleagues from the same culture – be it a national, ethnic or organisational culture – is rooted in a shared context and is usually based on a shared interest, often unspoken. For example, in an organisation, this shared interest may be in making that part of the organisation successful.

When people cooperate across cultures, it may well be necessary for them to work hard to define a shared context and to develop and maintain this shared interest, especially if local interests compete or conflict.

Building cooperation can be broken down into three phases.

Pre-contractual / Establishing contacts

Before we start to work together formally, for example in a joint venture or in a project team, we are likely to meet the people we are going to work with. Our judgements about people can sometimes be made very quickly – we like them or we don't like them; we think they are trustworthy or not.

We very quickly form these judgements on the basis of knowledge and experience we have gained – very often largely in our own cultural context. This might be a good guide when judging people from that context but it can easily let us down when we work internationally. In an unfamiliar context we need to be more flexible in our judgements. It can be wise to wait quite a while before you make up your mind about people who have very different backgrounds from your own.

Key Competence
Flexible judgement[1]

Not only flexible behaviour but also flexible judgement is a quality of effective international managers. They are flexible enough not to draw rapid and final conclusions about people and situations they don't know in cultures they don't know.
They are willing to question assumptions and stereotypes and revise their first impressions.

Relational

Having made contact with new people, we establish a basis for trusting cooperation through building relationships. And we build trusting relationships to a greater or lesser extent upon, for example, judgements about a person's:

> integrity. Can I trust that the person will behave in accordance
>   with a moral code?
> competence. Can I trust that the person will do his / her job or
>   perform a task well?
> consistency. Can I trust that he / she will behave in a way I can predict?
> openness with information. Can I trust that the person will share information
>   with me in the same way as I share information with him /her?

> reciprocity. Can I trust that he / she will help me in the same way as I help him / her?
> hospitality. Can I trust that he / she will look after me in the same way as I look after him / her?

In some national cultures, these last two elements are key. Trust comes when you join the 'in-group' and this may only happen if you show reciprocity and hospitality.

And you have to allow time for people (in the Middle East) to get to know you, your personality, if they can trust you or not. But when you are accepted you are very rapidly taken into the circle and then you are invited to lunch and dinner ... and things really speed up. When you are a member of the circle, it's at a very emotional level that you deal with people. Decisions are then emotionally based, not fact-based as we are used to.

Thomas Ruckdäsche (Germany), T-Systems, Germany

Structural

The third basis for cooperation is formal and has a mandatory character. The basis for cooperation on this level is, for example, a contract, the authority of the law and organisational procedures and processes. Members of some cultures share a strong belief in this element of cooperation. They believe that rules and contracts regulate behaviour in a relationship and are there to be followed for the good of everyone.

On the other hand, members of some cultures do not share such a strong belief in the supreme authority of law: perhaps there is no adequate legal system in place or maybe it is corrupt. They tend to believe that there are times when you must obey the letter of the law or a contract but that there are other times when you can ignore it, try to modify it or get round it. These cultures rely much more strongly on relationships based on trust – a handshake rather than a legal contract.

Regulating cooperation | 10.2

In *universalist* cultures,[2] there is a shared belief that codes and rules – for example, the rule of law, a moral or ethical code, a code of conduct or a contract – should regulate behaviour in relationships and society. These are seen as definitive and exceptions are not really acceptable as they tend to weaken the fundamental system of regulating behaviour. Examples of universalist cultures are the USA and north-west European countries. Protestant cultures tend to be universalist.

The consequences of a universalist tendency in business are predictable. Contracts have great significance, as do lawyers when business people draw up the contracts, and law courts when things go badly. For universalists, the contract regulates business expectations and behaviour.

In international management, the desire to systematise becomes stronger and stronger as a company grows larger and more complex: universal, standardised processes are the result. Codes of conduct describing a model of behaviour to be followed in an organisation acquire great importance not least because they also embody aspects of the law. Rules generated by an international project team also take on mandatory status for universalists.

In *particularist* cultures, the obligations people have to each other tend to regulate their behaviour towards each other. What Fons Trompenaars[3] describes as 'the exceptional nature of present circumstances' becomes more important than impersonal codes and rules. Examples of particularist cultures can be found in southern Europe and the Middle East. Cultures influenced by Roman Catholicism tend to be more particularist.

To particularists, relationships are extremely important in business and management because cooperation takes place most reliably with somebody whom you know and trust. To a particularist, a reliable business person is one who is prepared to take account of changing circumstances in a personal business relationship, for example by more readily modifying agreements and contracts.

Universalist cultures	Particularist cultures
Trust placed in codes, systems and models	Trust placed in networks of relationships
People are assigned to tasks	Tasks are assigned to people
Core business focus	Flexible customer focus
Standardisation and globalisation	Customisation and localisation
Fairness and consistency	Particular circumstances
Transparency and simplification	Appropriateness and contextualisation
Objective measurement of performance	Subjective measurement of performance
Facts convince	Opinions convince
The science of management	The art of management

Adapted from Trickey and Ewington (2003)

Building a common culture to take advantage of diversity | 10.3

When you start working internationally, in a project team or perhaps on an assignment, you need to start by exploring the diversity – the differences in the team. As you go on, you need to establish a common culture. This new orientation system should not view the differences in the team merely as difficulties to be managed but as a potential to be harnessed for the success of the task.

Leadership

The most influential factor in forming a common culture is the behaviour of management. International managers must demonstrate through their behaviour what they believe in. This means that they need a strong set of values which support their behaviour and are communicated to everybody they meet. The values of honesty, transparency and modesty are key values which need to shine out.

Of course, leaders needs to have other qualities such as drive, intelligence and an ability to build successful relationships. These help leaders to convince their colleagues that they have the competence to do the job.

Key competence
Personal autonomy through inner purpose[1]

Effective international managers often have a clear set of beliefs and values which gives them support in cultural environments which may be difficult to handle. These personal values can make them self-disciplined, confident and determined in achieving their goals. They provide them with a sense of purpose and direction, which they pass on to others.

Communication

Leaders need to put in place a strong platform for communicating across cultures. The first step is to agree a common language – usually English. Whatever language the company or the team chooses as a lingua franca, learning and using a few sentences in other languages demonstrates openness and respect for other cultures and people. It will help you in your relationship building in the team. Do not worry about not being fluent or feel embarrassed by your mistakes.

Key competence
Learning Languages[1]

Effective international managers have often been able to learn a number of different languages – especially when they are not native speakers of English. They win the appreciation of their local partners by learning and trying out a few sentences in their language. They enjoy learning and using their foreign languages.

You should never underestimate the barriers that language can create. Some unpublished research of our own at an international company has shown that about a third of problems encountered by international managers can be ascribed to language, a third to culture and a third to task complexity. Investment in a professional language learning programme is therefore essential for cooperating internationally. Another helpful step is to create a glossary of key terms used in the company (financial, technical, commercial, etc.).

In the past we had some meetings where we gave some clear definitions, a clear terminology. Depending on different countries we have different names for our products, so nobody knew which product people were talking about. So we decided that for this product we use this name. For this reporting, we all use this format. So when people did market research and gave information on market share, etc., to avoid the problem of comparing different types of data, it's important to specify the issue, market share in volumes or percentages, which columns for figures, etc. This makes communication clearer.

Camillo Mazzola (Italy), Henkel, Germany

However, even when people have attained an operational level in the common language, there can still be many communication breakdowns. The cause? People are often not willing to admit that they don't understand. Leaders need to work hard to optimise communication – for example, agreed best practice for email, telephone, video conferencing and meetings helps to make communication more effective.

Exchange

People working internationally need to see what it is really like to work in another country. Only when we live abroad do we really start to understand the host culture, our own culture, and other cultures too. Many companies have moved away from traditional expatriation – from head office to local markets – and instituted global exchange policies with people moving from local to local, local to head office and still sometimes head office to local. This demonstrates an attempt to take advantage of the diversity that is present in their workforce – as does working in cross-functional and cross-border teams.

Exchange is not just a question of physically moving location. It is also about providing opportunities for knowledge exchange. Knowledge about markets, products and cultures needs to be shared for an organisation to take advantage of the diversity. Developing a knowledge transfer process, supported by a company intranet, is another key building block in constructing a common culture.

Best practice
Cooperating in virtual teams | 10.4

International teams work virtually most of the time. Although the team shares a common goal, it does not share the same office, building or even country. The absence of face-to-face contact means that it is potentially more difficult for team members to cooperate. There are some key elements that you need in place.

Communication channels
> Face to face

Maximise any opportunity for face-to-face contact. Use the opportunity to meet socially as well as professionally as this will cement relationships. It will make for better communication once you are back in your local offices.

The kick-off meeting is a particularly important moment in the life of a virtual team. It may be one of the few moments when team members can spend time face to face. It is vital to maximise the use of this time.

Q: How important is the kick-off phase for an international team?
A: It's very, very important. When a team is not performing 100%, the main reasons are lack of time, lack of commitment and a badly prepared kick off. And yet sometimes we don't give enough focus to this.
Camillo Mazzola (Italy), Henkel, Germany

> **Email**
> Make sure you do not rely too much on email. Use email for information exchange but not for sensitive communication. Use it to book telephone calls as members of task- and time-oriented cultures may not cope well with unannounced telephone calls. Specify what is the expected response speed to emails (e.g. 24 or 48 hours).
> **Telephone**
> Use the telephone as your main one-to-one relationship-building medium. Especially with members of relationship-oriented or particularist cultures, it is important to telephone regularly and not just when you have something specific to say. Telephone calls are vital in keeping channels open.
> **Video conferences**
> Video conferences work well for top-down messages to the team with a chance for response and reaction from the team.
> **Communication platform**
> Make sure a shared technical platform is in place for data exchange, planning and communication.

Communication frequency
Make sure that you communicate frequently whether by email or by phone.

Communication processes
Plan telephone and video conferences well. They can be more efficient (but probably not more effective) than face-to-face meetings if everybody is well prepared. You need to structure the communication much more rigidly than in face-to-face meetings.

Feedback
Make sure you set up formal and informal feedback processes. It is very easy for motivation to drop or for priorities to change when people work virtually.

Cooperating in international teams | 10.5

Whether you are a team-member or a team-leader you will need to be mindful not only of your tasks but also of the other people in the team.

Tasks

> Giving direction (see Chapter 4)
A key driver for cooperation is the commitment to common goals. Sometimes the immediate objective – for example, to reduce costs in your region – can be very difficult to accept. You will only get commitment from local managers if they understand and are part of the larger goal – for example, to build market share in their region.

> Organisation and change (see Chapter 5)
In many organisations, projects are the main tool for driving through change. International project managers cannot assume that a head office project will be well accepted locally. They need to address local resistance to change and to involve and engage all parties in a process which is SMART – Specific, Measurable, Achievable, Relevant and Timely.

> Clarifying roles (see Chapter 6)
It is very important for everybody to be clear about their role and that of other team members. You cannot give support or ask for support unless you know what people do and what knowledge they have. It is vital to invest time at the start of an international project in specifying and clarifying roles.

> Understanding networks (see Chapter 6)
To get cooperation, team members also need to understand the networks which operate in the different parts of the world. This is not easy as it takes time. Drawing up a network diagram to show your colleagues who are the key members of your network is a good starting point. If you all do this, you should start to see where the networks overlap and also major gaps in the network.

People

> Communication (see Chapter 7)
Team members can feel very isolated when working internationally. They may also feel they are a long way from where the important decisions are being made. As a result they may start to think of themselves as small pawns in a much larger game of chess. Leaders need to work hard to communicate clearly, openly and frequently with their team and extended network. They need to understand the high probability of misunderstandings and use all means possible to make sure that people do understand each other.

> Handling feedback (see Chapter 8)
We have identified feedback as a basic human need. So you need to establish how you are going to build this into your daily practice. When working internationally it is difficult to see people do things and then comment on them. So you need to encourage reflection and ask your team members what

is going well and what is not. Involvement with the local management team will help in making feedback relevant to the local situation.

> Dealing with conflict (see Chapter 9)
Mindful international managers need to be prepared for conflict and consider their own attitude towards it. You need a set of strategies to deal with conflict which you can apply according to the situation, the person and the culture.

Effective cooperation consists not only of working together well but also seeing the benefit of being open to sharing different knowledge, experience and also difficulties.

Key Competence
Valuing differences[1]

Effective international managers enjoy working with people different from themselves. They find cultural diversity interesting and valuable and are sensitive to the different perspectives on the world that it creates. They are actively interested in understanding others' values, beliefs and practices and are able to communicate respect for them.

Having understood your differences, you then need to build a common culture which allows you to cooperate successfully and leverage the differences. Your empathy enables you to see things from other viewpoints and to recognise that the cultural diversity present in a group offers the potential for high performance.

And what is more, you have the ability to tap into this diversity to help the group create new solutions and options which may be more than the sum of the parts: 2 + 2 = 5!

Key Competence
Synergy through creating new alternatives[1]

Effective international managers are aware that it is necessary to take a systematic approach to getting the most out of international teams. It doesn't just happen by itself! They work at bringing out, understanding and reconciling the different cultural perspectives in the group and at using this potential to create genuinely new alternatives.

Notes

1
One of the Worldwork international competency set.
2
See Parsons (1937).
3
See Trompenaars (1993).

References

1
Adler, Nancy (2002). *International Dimensions of Organizational Behavior. 4th ed.* Cincinnati: South-Western College Publishing.

2
Bennett, Milton (1995). Critical Incidents in an Intercultural Conflict-Resolution Exercise. In: Fowler, Sandra M. and Monica G. Mumford (Ed.). *Intercultural Sourcebook: Cross-Cultural Training Methods* Vol. 1: 147–156. Yarmouth: Intercultural Press.

3
Blanchard, Ken, Patricia Zigarmi and Drea Zigarmi (1986). *Leadership and the One-Minute Manager.* London: Collins.

4
Burgess, S. and J.-B.E.M. Steenkamp (1999). Value Priorities and Consumer Behaviour in a Transitional Economy. In: Batra, R. (Ed.). *Marketing Issues in Transitional Economies*: 85–105. Boston: Kluwer.

5
Cottle, T.J. (1967). The Circles Test: an investigation of perception of temporal relatedness and dominance. *Journal of Projective Technique and Personality Assessment* 31, 5: 58–71.

6
Davidov, Eldad (2008). A Cross-Country and Cross-Time Comparison of Human Values Measurements with the Second Round of the European Social Survey. *Survey Research Methods* Vol. 2, No. 1: 33–46.

7
Distefano, Joseph J. and Martha L. Maznevski (2000). Creating Value with Diverse Teams in Global Management. *Organizational Dynamics* Vol. 29, 1: 45–63.

8
French, W. L. and C. H. Bell, (1979). *Organization Development.* Englewood Cliffs, NJ: Prentice Hall.

9
Gudykunst, William B. (2004). *Bridging Differences. Effective Intergroup Communication. 4th Edition.* Thousand Oaks: Sage.

10
Hall, Edward T. (1959). *The Silent Language.* Garden City, New York: Doubleday.

11
Hall, Edward T. (1966). *The Hidden Dimension.* New York: Doubleday.

12
Hall, Edward T. (1976). *Beyond Culture.* Garden City, New York: Anchor Press/ Doubleday.

13
Hersey, Paul (1985). *Situational Selling: An Approach for Increasing Sales Effectiveness.* Escondido: Center for Leadership Studies.

14
Hersey, Paul, Kenneth H. Blanchard and Dewey E. Johnson (2001). *Management of Organizational Behavior: Leading Human Resources, 8th Edition.* Upper Saddle River: Prentice Hall.

15
Hofstede, Geert (1980, 2001). *Culture's Consequences: Comparing Values, Behaviors, Institutions, and Organizations Across Nations. 2nd Edition.* Thousand Oaks: Sage.

16
Hofstede, Geert (1994). *Cultures and Organisations: Software of the Mind*. London: McGraw-Hill.

17
Kluckhohn, Florence Rockwood and Fred L. Strodtbeck (1961). *Variations in Value Orientations*. New York: Harper & Row.

18
Langer, Ellen J. (1989). *Mindfulness*. Reading: Addison-Wesley.

19
Langer, Ellen J. (1997). *The Power of Mindful Learning*. Reading, MA: Addison-Wesley.

20
Laurent, Andre (1986). The Cross-Cultural Puzzle of International Human Resource Management. *Human Resource Management* Vol. 25, 1: 91–102.

21
LeBaron, Michelle and Bruce Grundison (1993). *Conflict and Culture: Research in Five Communities in British Columbia, Canada*. Victoria: University of Victoria Institute for Dispute Resolution.

22
Lewin, Kurt (1936). Some social-psychological differences between the US and Germany. *Journal of Personality* Vol.4, 4: 265–29.

23
Lewin, Kurt (1936). *Principles of Topological Psychology*. New York: MacGraw-Hill.

24
Luft, Joseph and Harry Ingham (1955). The Johari window, a graphic model of interpersonal awareness. *Proceedings of the Western Training Laboratory in Group Development*. Los Angeles: U.C.L.A. Extension Office.

25
Margerison, Charles and Dick McCann (1992). *Team Management Profile Handbook*. York: Prado Systems.

26
Margerison, Charles and Dick McCann (1995). *Team Management: Practical New Approaches*. Chalford: Management Books 2000 Ltd.

27
Margerison, Charles and Dick McCann (1997). *High Energy Teams Workbook*. Milton, QLD: Team Management Systems.

28
Markus, H. and S. Kitayama (1991). Culture and Self : Implications for cognition, emotion, and motivation. *Psychological Review* 2: 224–253.

29
Markus, H. and S. Kitayama (1994). A collective fear of the collective: Implications for selves and theories of selves. *Personality and Social Psychology Bulletin* 20: 568–579.

30
Parsons, Talcott (1937). *The Structure of Social Action*. New York: McGraw-Hill.

31
Parsons, Talcott and Edward Shils (1951). *Towards a General Theory of Action*. Cambridge: Harvard University Press.

32
Ruhly, Sharon (1976). *Orientations to Intercultural Communication*. Palo Alto, Calif.: Science Research Associates.

33
Schein, Edgar (1985, 2004). *Organizational Culture and Leadership, 3rd Edition*. San Francisco: Jossey-Bass.

34
Schwartz, Shalom (1999). A theory of cultural values and some implications for work. *Applied Psychology: An International Review* 48(1): 23–47.

35
Schwartz, Shalom H. and Anat Bardi (2001). Value hierarchies across cultures. *Journal of Cross-Cultural Psychology* 32(3): 268–290.

36
Schwartz, S.H., G. Melech, A. Lehmann, S. Burgess, M. Harris and V. Owens (2001). Extending the cross-cultural validity of the theory of basic human values with a different method of measurement. *Journal of Cross-Cultural Psychology* Vol. 32, No. 5: 519–542.

37
Schwartz, Shalom H. (1992). Universals in the content and structure of values: theoretical advances and empirical tests in 20 countries. In: Zanna, Mark P. (Ed.). *Advances in Experimental Social Psychology* Vol. 25: 1–65. San Diego: Academic Press.

38
Schwartz, Shalom H. (1994). Beyond individualism/collectivism: New dimensions of values. In: Kim, U., H. C. Triandis, C. Kagiticibasi, S. Choi, and G. Yoon (Eds.). *Individualism and Collectivism: Theory, Methods and Applications*. Thousand Oaks: Sage.

39
Schwartz, S.H., A. Lehmann and S. Roccas (1999). Multimethod Probes of Basic Human Values. In: Adamopulous, J. and Y. Kashima (Eds.). *Social Psychology and Cultural Context: Essays in Honor of Harry C. Triandis*: 107–123. Newbury Park: Sage.

40
Spencer-Oatey, Helen and Peter Franklin (forthcoming). *Intercultural Interaction. A Multi-Disciplinary Approach to Intercultural Communication*. London: Palgrave Macmillan.

41
The Chinese Culture Connection (Eds.) (1987). Chinese values and the search for culture-free dimensions of culture. *Journal of Cross-Cultural Psychology* Vol.18, 2: 143–174.

42
Thomas, Kenneth W. (1976). Conflict and conflict management. In: Dunnette, Marvin D. (Ed.). *Handbook of Industrial and Organizational Psychology*: 889–935. Chicago: Rand NcNally.

43
Thomas, David C. and Kerr Inkson (2003). *Cultural Intelligence. People Skills for Global Business*. San Francisco: Berrett-Koehler.

44
Ting-Toomey, Stella (1999). *Communicating Across Cultures*. New York: The Guilford Press.

45
Trickey, David and Nigel Ewington (2003). *A World of Difference. Working Successfully Across Cultures*. London: Capita Learning and Development.

46
Trompenaars, Fons (1993). *Riding the Waves of Culture: Understanding Cultural Diversity in Business.* Chicago: Irwin.

47
Verluyten, S. Paul (1999). Conflict avoidance in Thailand. Paper presented at Eleventh ENCoDe Conference: *International negotiation: communication across business cultures.* Barcelona.

48
Weaver, G. and P. Uncapher (1981). *The Nigerian experience: Overseas living and value change.* Paper presented at the Seventh Annual SIETAR Conference, Vancouver, B.C., Canada.

49
Zaninelli, Susanne (1994). Vier Schritte eines integrativen, Trainingsansatzes am Beispiel eines interkulturellen Trainings: Deutschland – U S A. In: *Materialien zum internationalen Kulturaustausch* 33: 5–8. Stuttgart: Institut für Auslandsbeziehungen.

Profiles of the managers quoted

The authors would like to thank all the interviewees for their contributions to this book. We have managed to collect together short profiles of most of them. Our apologies go to those whose profiles are missing.

Brian Cracknell is the Director of Language Works, Malaysia, where he has lived for the last 29 years. He designs and delivers innovative learning experiences for clients throughout South East Asia.

John Duncan is a business language and communication teacher of many years' standing. He has worked in Libya, Egypt, and Finland, and spent eight years as a teacher-trainer in Hong Kong. He has written twelve English language and communication textbooks.

Birgitta Gregor worked internationally in human resource management positions in industry for many years. As a management consultant her projects include change processes and organisation development in Europe and Africa.

Erik Hallberg presently heads the Swedish Broadband Services operations of the Swedish telecoms company TeliaSonera. During his nine years with the company, Erik also headed up its Baltic operations. Earlier in his career, Erik worked as CEO of a European telecoms company and established a new operation for alternative telecom in 8 countries.

Ulrich Hansen is currently Manager of Process and Plant Safety at Henkel in Dusseldorf. In his career he has worked in Milan, Paris and Saudi Arabia. In his current role he acts as an internal consultant travelling worldwide to support production sites.

Dr. Frank Kühn worked in the electrical industry and in research institutions, where he was responsible for labour economics and organization. As a partner at HLP Hirzel Leder & Partner he supports executives and teams in developing their international organizations in the areas of project management, process management and interaction.

Wibke Kuhnert worked for five years in consulting before she joined Henkel in 2004. There she led an international team responsible for design and implementation of standard finance processes in the US and Europe. She has recently moved to the operational business and is leading the Business Controlling department of Henkel Cosmetics Retail in Germany.

Camillo Mazzola is currently Marketing Director at Henkel Italy Consumer Adhesives. He has considerable international experience not only in Henkel but also with Loctite, Duracell and Nestlé.

Washington Munetsi is an international human resources practioner, working for Nestlé, the largest food and beverages company in the world based in Vevey, Switzerland.

Luis Ortega has held different positions in purchasing at Henkel. After an assignment in Turkey he was appointed Corporate Manager of Plastic Packaging for the Personal Care Division.

Lorenzo Pestalozzi is a director of CRPM, a leading training organization in western Switzerland. He is a Swiss citizen, with international experience in sales and marketing and executive management positions.

Dani Razmgah has worked as Competence Manager, Director of Project Management and he is now Human Resource Manager at Swedbank. He has many years of experience of management. He also works as a management consultant and is the founder of the Swedish Management Academy. He works mostly in Sweden, Scandinavia and in the Baltic States, but also in the Middle East and to a lesser extent in the UK.

Tim Taylor has worked in consumer products R&D for Unilever, Reckitt-Benckiser, and Henkel (both in Germany and at their subsidiary, The Dial Corporation, in Arizona). Tim is currently a Director in the R&D department at Dial.

Peter Wollmann has worked in numerous international projects in the last few years at Zurich Financial Services, one of the leading international insurance companies. Since 2005 he has been Head of Strategic Business Development at Zurich Group Germany with functions in the worldwide Zurich matrix organisation. He is also co-publisher and author of several books on 'project management'

Index

The numbers refer to the section or sections in which the term or the author's work is primarily dealt with.

Glossary

This glossary describes the meaning of the words listed as they are used in the book and not in all their possible meanings.

360° feedback: feedback on an employee from a wide variety of sources, such as your bosses, subordinates, and colleagues. Sometimes it also includes feedback from the person herself. The feedback is usually given anonymously.

accommodation: giving up your own interests to satisfy those of the other person in a conflict. See also: appeasement.

affirmative feedback: affirmative feedback tells people what they did well, often also involving praise and even rewards.

ambiguity: a state or situation which can be viewed and interpreted in several ways and is therefore unclear and confusing.

appeasement: a strategy which gives in to demands or orders in order to maintain good and harmonious relationships at the expense of your own interests. See also: accommodation.

appraisal: an assessment or judgment of something; an evaluation of the abilities of an employee; a formal process of giving feedback on an employees' performance.

appropriate: suitable for a particular situation.

assertive: very self-confident, direct and confident when interacting with others; determined in a conflict situation.

assumption: something which is taken for granted, something which is believed without requiring proof; an idea of how things or people are like without really knowing whether that idea is true.

autonomy: being independent of others, making decisions by yourself and not being influenced by others.

avoidance: in terms of conflict management strategies, if you use an avoidance strategy you are not interested either in giving in to others or in satisfying your own interests.

benevolence: being kind, nice and caring to people, wanting to help people and care for their well-being, wanting to do good to others.

blocker: something which blocks and hinders a process, e.g. change; something which prevents a process from being carried forward and which weakens the process; see also: driver (opposite).

to blur: making it difficult to see the clear lines and boundaries of a situation or thing; to become unclear and indistinct.

bottom-up: interaction or processes starting at the bottom of the hierarchy in an organization and moving upwards; employees giving suggestions and other input to leaders which is then transported up the organizational hierarchy and finally judged by those leaders. See also: top-down (opposite).

boundary: the borders or limits of something; a concept defining your responsibilities and task within a team or organization.

buy-in: everything that somebody can contribute to a team or organization and its success; acceptance, for example, of the value statement of an organization and being willing to act according to that statement.

to cement: cementing a position or relationship means to emphasize or strengthen it.

code of conduct: rules and regulations on how to act and behave in a certain situation or in a certain organization.

conform: to follow and act according to the rules, norms and regulations set by an organization; to act as you are expected to act.

conservation: conservation is a set of value orientations originated by Shalom H. Schwartz which is made up of the values of conformity, security and tradition. Scoring high on conservation means that it is likely that you follow rules, avoid danger, and find religion and customs important.

consistency: acting or behaving in a similar way in similar situations and contexts over time, without strong changes in behaviour or performance.

context: the circumstances in which a particular event takes place; the setting and a set of characteristics of a particular event; the set of characteristics that form the setting for a situation and therefore enables people to interpret it in a particular way.

contextualize: to place something in a particular context in order to understand it better; see also: context.

culture-blind: not being able to see the characteristics of a culture other than your own; not being aware that people of a different culture communicate or act differently. See also: culture-sensitive (opposite).

culture-sensitive: being capable of seeing the characteristics of a culture other than your own; being aware that people of a different culture communicate or act differently. See also: culture-blind (opposite).

deep-seated: firmly established. Deep-seated ideas, concepts and feelings are very difficult to change or adapt. Sometimes, people are unaware of these deep-seated ideas, concepts and feelings.

defensive: if the members of a group become defensive towards others, they try to exclude them and may not share information freely with them. They may try to hide their weaknesses and protect their own interests.

deference: openly showing respect to people more powerful than yourself; showing submission and respect to others because of their age, status or position.

to delayer: if you delayer an organization, you get rid of some of the hierarchical levels in order to make the whole system flatter, thereby making interaction between people from various levels easier and more direct.

detriment: to the detriment of something or somebody means that somebody or something suffers a disadvantage; at the expense of something; the state of being damaged or made worse.

developmental feedback: feedback from a manager who evaluates an individual or a team which is not performing as well as expected, with the aim of helping the individual or team to perform better and reach their objectives; feedback which aims to lead to a change of behaviour and performance for the better.

discreet: carefully communicating or doing something with the aim or keeping it confidential and trying to avoid embarrassing others.

domination: in conflict management, domination is an orientation in which somebody who is involved in a conflict tries to succeed and get his / her own way at all costs.

down-toner: a word or expression which takes away some of the directness and strength of what is communicated – the meaning of the message is not changed, but it is seen as less imposing by the receiver of it.

driver: something which helps and supports a process, e.g. change; something which carries a process forward and strengthens it.

to embody: to include, to contain; to be an expression of an idea, concept or feeling.

to escalate: to make more intense and serious.

explicit: clearly expressed, formulated or stated; not hidden; see also: implicit (opposite).

to exploit: to make full use of something; to use something as well as possible in order to get the most out of it.

extrovert: a person who is confident, relaxed and at ease in a social environment. See also: introvert (opposite).

face: if you lose face, you lose your dignity and you feel embarrassed or ashamed.

face value: if you take a comment or feedback at face value, you accept the apparent and obvious meaning, even though the real and hidden meaning may be different.

feudal: referring to the system of feudalism: in a figurative sense, it means here that lower-ranking people support higher-ranking people without questioning whether what the higher-ranking people do is right or wrong.

fit in: if you fit in easily in a group, you are accepted and considered to be a valuable member of this group, and you and your values are unlikely to cause any conflict within that group.

gate-keepers: a person who controls access to something or someone.

generalist: a generalist education is an education that strongly values a general and broad education; a person who is competent in many areas and who can do a lot of different things but at a lower level of competence than a specialist.

glue: in a figurative sense, something which holds various parts together; a common understanding between people which holds these people together and connects them more.

guanxi: a concept in Chinese society which describes the social network of friends, acquaintances, colleagues and others who have various responsibilities and roles in that network.

hands-off: having a hands-off role means that people are not directly involved in working with their colleagues and staff. They leave their staff to do the job alone without detailed instruction.

harness: using something for a particular advantageous purpose.

hearsay: rumours or something which you have heard from somebody but the truth of which you cannot check; information about somebody which you have received from others and not from that person directly.

hedonism: an attitude which aims at getting as much fun and pleasure as possible in life and trying to enjoy it.

hierarchy: a system in which members of an organization are ranked according to their status; a hierarchy reflects the power relationships within an organization.

hospitality: the condition of being friendly and welcoming to others; in a business context, entertaining business partners or clients in order to promote harmonious relationships.

implicit: understood but not directly expressed, clear or observable; see also: explicit (opposite).

individualism: the concept of people seeing themselves as individuals acting independently from others without feeling that strong obligations exist between people.

in-group: a group of people sharing similar interests and similar characteristics; people with whom you are in close contact because you share a similar identity; see also: out-group (opposite).

integrity: the condition of being honest and having strong moral convictions.

interdependent: being dependent on each other; feeling that you have strong obligations towards other members of a group and that your identity is shaped by the interaction with other members of a group.

interlocutor: the person you are talking to.

interplay: the way in which several things or people depend and have an effect of each other.

introvert: person who is not confident and not at ease in a social environment and somebody who is primarily concerned with their own feelings rather than the world about them; see also: extrovert (opposite).

kick-off: the start of an event or meeting, often allowing time for team members to get to know each other.

line function: the function that an employee has in an organization in his / her day-to-day job as opposed to the particular role and function he / she plays while working in a specially formed project team.

lingua franca: a language which is used by members of an organization who work together but who speak different languages – in international business, English is very often the lingua franca.

loyalty: the quality of showing strong and constant support to others, usually over a long period of time.

majority culture: a culture which dominates or is very powerful; a culture whose members make up the majority of the number of people in a society; see also: minority culture (opposite).

mandatory: required and not optional; compulsory.

mentor: an experienced person in an organization who helps new employees and guides them in their career and their work and gives them advice on both work-related and personal issues.

to micro-manage: to manage in a very detailed manner.

mindset: the set of attitudes and ways of behavior typical of a group.

minefield: in a figurative sense, a minefield is a potentially dangerous and unclear situation; in a cultural minefield, people do not know where there may be potential problems in communicating or interacting with others and whether they may even insult others without being aware of it.

minority culture: a culture which is more open to outer influences than members of the majority culture; see also: majority culture (opposite).

mission statement: a formal and written statement of the aims, values and attitudes of an organization; it outlines what the organization wants to do and achieve and how it wants to do and achieve this.

modesty: behaviour in which you avoid talking about your knowledge and skills; not boasting about your skills

non-verbal: non-verbal communication is communication without using words or speech; smiling, nodding and other features of body language are examples of ways to communicate in a non-verbal way.

other-centred: attaching more importance to the interests of other people than to your own.

outcome: result.

outgoing: friendly and confident in a social environment.

out-group: a group of people with which you do not share similar interests; people with whom you are not in close contact; see also: in-group (opposite).

to overlap: if two systems, actions or ideas overlap, they involve some of the same periods of time, topics or people; taking place at the same time.

pace: the speed or rhythm at which an organization works and at which organizational processes take place; a single step when walking.

particularist: for a particularist, personal relationships are very important for doing business, because they emphasize the importance of trust in a business setting; for particularists, a particular relationship in a business context is more important than abstract rules according to which an organization functions; see also: universalist (opposite).

to peer coach: to train or advise colleagues.

prevent: to keep something from happening; to stop someone from doing something.

predictable: able to be foreseen; if something is predictable, people can assume that it will happen as they expect it to happen, even if they cannot be sure of this.

prejudice: an unreasonable dislike of something, an opinion or assessment that is not based on actual experience and first-hand knowledge or insights; see also: stereotype.

psychometric: relating to measuring mental processes or capacities; relating to measuring an individual's personality or behaviour.

reciprocity: the practice of helping each other so that there is benefit for everyone involved.

relational: concerning the relationship between people interacting together rather than the task-related aspects of their interaction.

reliable: if somebody is reliable, you can trust that that person will act as you expects him / her to act; performing consistently well.

to reprimand: to express disapproval and dissatisfaction with somebody in a formal way.

resentment: a feeling of bitterness and anger towards others.

to resolve: to find a solution to a problem or conflict.

to restrain: to keep low; to keep under control; to keep well within limits.

to ridicule: to make fun of somebody, to make others laugh at somebody.

to root: to come from; to base something on; to originate from.

rudimentary: not strongly developed or basic; relatively simple or even too simple.

rungs on the ladder: steps of a ladder; in a figurative sense, each rung on the ladder symbolizes one hierarchical level within an organization: if you go up the ladder step-by-step, you rise in the organizational hierarchy.

sceptical: not being convinced easily, having doubts about something.

self-centred: attaching more importance to your own interests than to those of others.

self-reliant: counting on yourself and your own capabilities rather than on others; wanting not to be dependent on others.

silo mentality: the characteristic way of thinking of the members of an organization that categorizes people or procedures into boxes, denying that it is important to take into account the relationships and interactions between these boxes.

sincerity: the quality of being honest with people; the quality of not deceiving people; the quality of not manipulating people to your own advantage.

stakeholder: a person, group, or organisation who affects or can be affected by an organisation's actions.

stereotype: an image or idea of a particular person or group of people which is fixed and not easily changed and which oversimplifies the characteristics of that person or group of people; see also: prejudice.

substantive: important and meaningful; not superficial.

subtle: relatively precise, varied and detailed rather than relatively unfocused or general.

to surface: to make explicit and not allow to remain hidden and unspoken; to describe or articulate something.

to take for granted: if you take something for granted, you assume it just has to be like that and that it cannot be otherwise.

to take turns: to begin to speak in a conversation.

to talk down: if you talk down to people, you give them the impression that you are more important or knowledgeable than they are.

tangible: real; having the quality of being seen or recognized; considerable.

to throw off: to abandon something; to discontinue something; to leave something behind; to get rid of something.

to tick the box: if you tick the boxes, you complete something or you do something because you are required to do it rather than because you see a real need to do it; following a particular process because you have to rather than because you believe in it.

top-down: interaction or procedures starting at the top of the hierarchy in an organization and moving downwards; the leader decides without taking into account suggestions from employees and then communicates her decision down the hierarchy; see also: bottom-up (opposite)

transactional: concerning the task-related aspects of people's interaction rather than the relationship between the people interacting together.

transversal: cutting across the usual hierarchical or functional lines. If people from various hierarchies and from various departments work together for a particular purpose, often in project teams, you speak of a transversal structure.

trustworthy: if somebody is trustworthy, you can rely on them to be honest. If a person is trustworthy, we trust him / her and believe he / she will do what she has promised to do.

uncertainty: the state of doubt or being unsure about the future and about what is the right thing to do; the state of feeling threatened by unclear or unknown situations.

to underpin: to support and strengthen something by providing a robust foundation.

universalist: for a universalist, formal rules and regulations determine behaviour and interaction with others – these codes and rules are seen as definitive and exceptions are not really considered to be acceptable, not even with close and trusted business partners; see also: particularist (opposite).

virtual: virtual teams are teams which are not located in the same office or in nearby buildings – such teams are spread geographically and often work together using e-mail and other Internet applications.

work-life balance: the principle that work should be in proportion to private life in order to take into account the need for rest and recreation of employees and thus support their well-being.